A Taste of Lorrha

A Taste of Lorrha

Baking with Love

by the Friends and Residents of Lorrha, Co. Tipperary

THP
TIGH HATTIE PRESS

Published in 2021 by
Tigh Hattie Press
tighhattiepress@gmail.com

First Edition

Editor: David J Hewitt

ISBN-979 8 53371 665 9

To the **SCÉAL** committee and its fundraising project
facilitating the build of an extension to the Lorrha Community Hall,
aimed at providing a dedicated shop and café for the benefit of the local
community and visitors alike.

Contents

Welcome

Nestling in the gentle hills of north Tipperary, strategically placed close to the mighty River Shannon, is the monastic village of Lorrha. Its very existence goes back to the middle of the first millennium, when Lorrha would have been sought out not only for spiritual guidance, but as a refuge offering food and shelter. With the connection to St Ruadhán, visits to Lorrha would almost certainly been a pilgrimage for those on their own spiritual journey.

Within the parish of Lorrha and Dorrha, the village has evolved over the last 1,500 years and today stands proud amidst the remains of three religious sites. Just as the monks would have welcomed travellers to Lorrha, the same essence of hospitality holds true today: you will be welcomed in that same spirit of community with a "Hello, you are most welcome!", ensuring that our visitors do not forget their experience of the village.

The purpose behind this book is to avoid that happening and the clue is in the title. Through these pages, it is our hope that you recall your visit to Lorrha through the dual meanings of the word "Taste": we offer you recipes submitted by local people, some of which recall the favourite baking of previous generations or the influence of those with foreign connections now resident in the parish; we also offer you the briefest introduction to the historical side of our village. Although small in settlement, Lorrha is considerable in terms of its contribution to the multi-faceted history of Ireland.

Our hope is that in years to come, through the pages of this book, which has truly been a community effort, you will re-live your time in Lorrha, no matter how long or short your visit, and be pleasantly reminded of your experience.

S.C.É.A.L.

Social Community Enterprise
for the Advancement of Lorrha/Rathcabbin

Love Lorrha

Historic Monastic Village

www.visitlorrhadorrha.com

An Irish Kitchen Prayer

May we be blessed with good food,
the gift of great craic
and the sound of hearty laughter.

May we share
the love and joy of companionship
over a hearty meal
or a hot cuppa and a grand slice
every single day.

Amen

Aoibhie's Walnut Brown Bread

Contributed by Una, who says:

"Serve sliced on a breadboard with a pot of butter for spreading!
This is beautiful served as a treat with smoked salmon."

INGREDIENTS:

450g wholemeal flour
100g strong white flour
600mℓ buttermilk
25g light brown sugar
50g walnuts
2 tsp fine sea salt
2 tsp bread soda
2 tbsp treacle
2 tbsp rapeseed oil
2 tbsp pumpkin seeds for decoration

METHOD:

Pre-heat oven to 200°C / 350°F / Gas mark 4.
Grease 2 x 1 pint loaf tins

Sift the plain flour and bread soda into a bowl.
Then add the wholemeal flour, salt and sugar.
Combine everything thoroughly.

Make a well in the centre of the dry ingredients.
Add the buttermilk, treacle, rapeseed oil and walnuts.
Mix everything until well incorporated.

Divide the mixture evenly between the two greased loaf tins.
Sprinkle the pumpkin seeds on top of each filled tin.

Bake for approximately 40 minutes.
Check that the loaves are cooked by tapping the base of a loaf. It should sound hollow.

Once cooked, remove from the tins and allow to cool on a wire tray.

Enjoy!

Apple Sour Cream Cake with Honey

Contributed by Suzanne, who says:

"So easy and quick to make — it is delicious hot or cold. Serve as a dessert with cream or Greek yoghurt or on its own with a cup of tea."

INGREDIENTS:

450g eating apples, peeled and sliced
150g butter
Grated zest of 1 lemon
150g caster sugar (preferably golden)
150g sour cream or crème fraiche
150g self-raising flour
3 tbsp honey
1 large egg

METHOD:

Pre-heat oven to 180°C / 350°F / Gas mark 4.
Grease an 18cm / 7-inch deep tin.

Put the apple slices in a pan with 25g of the butter and gently sauté for 8 – 10 minutes until soft.
Remove from heat and stir in lemon zest (if you don't have any lemon zest, you can substitute some ground cinnamon or ground cloves).

Beat the remaining butter with the sugar.
When creamed, beat in the egg and add the sour cream/crème fraiche.
Mix until smooth, then fold in the flour followed by the apples.
Put into the prepared tin and smooth the top of the mixture.

Bake for approximately 1 hour (keep an eye on it after about ½ an hour). It is cooked when a cocktail stick or cake tester comes out clean when inserted into the middle of the cake.

Remove from the oven and leave the cake in the tin whilst preparing the honey.
Heat the honey gently in a pan.
Poke some holes in the cake and drizzle the warmed honey evenly over the surface.

Allow to cool before removing from the tin as the cake can sometimes be fragile.

Just to be safe, Suzanne recommends lining the tin with baking parchment.

Serve hot or cold with cream, ice cream or yoghurt.

Aunty Gerda's Meringue-Berry Cake

Contributed by Ute, who says:

"My Aunt Gerda in Germany bakes this cake for special occasions – I love the fresh, fruity, crunchy flavour."

INGREDIENTS (in 3 sections):

A:

125g butter (room temperature)
115g caster sugar
4 egg yolks
150g self-raising flour
3-5 tbsp milk

B:

4 egg whites
200g caster sugar
4-5 tbsp flaked almonds

C:

250g mascarpone
200mℓ fresh cream
150g yoghurt
75g caster sugar
1 tbsp vanilla sugar
3 tbsp lime or lemon juice
400g fresh strawberries,
         halved or quartered
         (or blueberries,
         raspberries or
         blackberries)

<u>METHOD</u> (in 3 steps):

A:

Using an electric mixer, beat the butter until creamy, then slowly add the sugar. When combined with the butter, add the 4 egg yolks and mix well. Lastly, gradually add the flour and, when mixed in, add the milk. You should now have a Madeira mixture, which slowly falls from a spoon when tested.

Divide the mixture between 2 well-greased 26cm / 10¼ inch spring-form cake tins and spread evenly.

B:

Beat the egg whites at medium speed until stiff then add caster sugar slowly, spoon by spoon, while beating at high speed to make a meringue mix.

Divide the meringue mixture and spoon it equally onto the two prepared, uncooked Madeira cake bases. Sprinkle the flaked almonds evenly over both meringue-topped mixtures.

Bake for about 30 minutes in a fan oven (not pre-heated) to 110°C. If the almonds have not browned by this time, bake for a further 5 minutes at 140°C.

Remove from oven and let cool for 10 minutes.

Carefully remove the baked cakes from the tins.

C:

Whilst the cakes are baking, prepare the filling.

Whisk the mascarpone, yoghurt, sugars and lime or lemon juice together until smooth. Lastly, carefully fold in the cream, which you have first whipped. Cover one of the completely cooled Madeira/meringue cakes with half the filling, add all the berries then cover with the second layer of filling.

Place the second cooled cake on top, meringue facing up.

Best enjoyed very fresh...yummy!

St Ruadhán: Early Monasticism

St Ruadhán, born during the early part of the sixth century, was to become a leading figure of the early Christian Church in Ireland. He founded an abbey in Lorrha in c.AD 540.

The original building, standing to the east of the village, would have been constructed from wood and surrounded by a large defensive mound. These were troubled times, so such a structure would have kept animals safely in and marauding bands of very unwelcome, warlike visitors out. This defensive mound is still visible in places today.

The original church was replaced with a stone structure in c.AD 1000. This is what you see today. The present Church of Ireland (built c.AD 1815) incorportes the eastern wall of this medieval stone church. There are the remains of two high crosses in the churchyard.

The monks would have followed the Rule of St Columbanus and their presence in Lorrha continued until c.AD 1100.

The lives of the brothers would have been hard, but simple, divided between worship and working to make the settlement self-sufficient in all aspects of its requirements. The trade and security afforded by such an established abbey probably gave rise to the growth of a surrounding secular settlement, which gradually became Lorrha village.

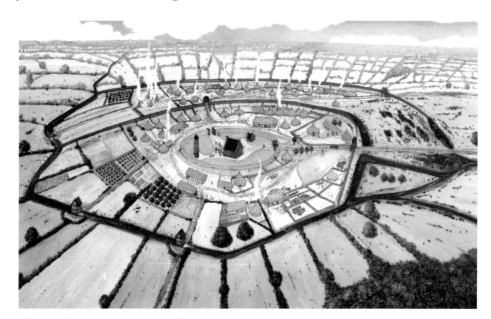

Famous for his prophecies, St Ruadhán is associated with the "Cursing of Tara", in which he predicted the manner of the death of Diarmait mac Cerbaill, King of Tara and High King of Ireland.

After his own death, St Ruadhán was revered as a saint and was regarded as one of the "Twelve Apostles of Ireland ". He is believed to have died in Lorrha on 15th April, AD 584, but the site of his burial is not known.

The illustrations are from information panels at the Community Hall and Church of Ireland locations.
Stained glass window of St Ruadhán (20th Century) from St Ruadhán's Roman Catholic Church, Lorrha.

Biscuit Fingers

Contributed by Marian, who admits:

"If you have a sweet tooth... delicious!"

INGREDIENTS:

3 Mars Bars or
3 Snickers Bars – you need a total of
                  about 3oz / 85g
3oz / 85g margarine
3oz / 85g Rice Krispies

METHOD:

Melt your chosen bars in a pan over a gentle heat.
When melted, stir in the Rice Krispies and mix well.

Line a Swiss roll tin with parchment paper.
Pour the mixture into the Swiss roll tin and flatten evenly.
Leave the mixture to cool and set.
When completely cooled, cut into fingers.

And for that extra treat...

As an option: before cutting the cooled mixture into fingers, melt some additional slab chocolate over a gentle heat and then spread it over the cooled biscuits.

Allow the chocolate to cool completely before cutting the finished chocolate-topped biscuit base into fingers.

Quick suggestion:
This is an easy recipe for the kids to make, but always under parental supervision.

Boiled Fruit Cake

Contributed by Ann, who says:

"My Mam used to make this delicious boiled fruit cake.
It was loved by us all."

INGREDIENTS:

225g Stork margarine
400ml milk
225g dark brown sugar
450g flour (sieved)
2 eggs
450g sultanas **or** 225g sultanas + 225g raisins

1 tsp mixed spice
½ tsp cinnamon
Pinch of salt
2 tsp bread soda

METHOD:

Pre-heat oven to 150°C / 300°F / Gas mark 2.
Line an 18cm / 7-inch tin with 2 layers of greaseproof paper, then wrap the outside of the tin with brown paper. Secure with string.

Put the margarine, milk, brown sugar and fruit in a pan and melt down very gently for about 15 minutes.
Remove the pan from the heat and allow to cool.

Beat the eggs and then stir them through the cooled mixture.
Keep back a little of the flour. Add the rest of the flour and spices.
Lastly, add the bread soda to the remaining flour, mix it well and then also add this to everything else.
Mix thoroughly.

Put the mixture into the prepared tin, cover the top of the cake with brown paper and bake for approximately 1½ hours.

Remove from oven when cooked.
Remove the brown paper and pour
a little whiskey over the top, if desired.

Quick tip:
Check the centre of the cake with a cake tester or skewer to ensure it's cooked...

Lorrha's Norman Motte

Following the arrival of the Normans in Ireland (AD 1169-AD 1171), it became necessary to erect fortifications at strategic spots across the land, mainly to ward off incursions by the indigenous Irish inhabitants. These structures were the so-called motte and bailey castles: the motte comprising a high earthen mound topped by a wooden tower, forming the lord's residence and final defence when under attack; the bailey being a surrounding enclosed perimeter space which was the main residential area.

This kind of structure was a sophisticated form of defence at the time and was cheap and easy to build – two important considerations for the Normans during their conquest of Ireland.

Lorrha's castle was situated close to the village, the parish church and the Lorrha River. It was built by John Marshal in AD 1207. In the following year it was destroyed by Murcliad Da Bria, but was later rebuilt. It is recorded again in AD 1212. Archaeological traces of the bailey remain, but the motte has been considerably eroded by time, the weather and human activity. However, part of the motte is still visible today (on private land).

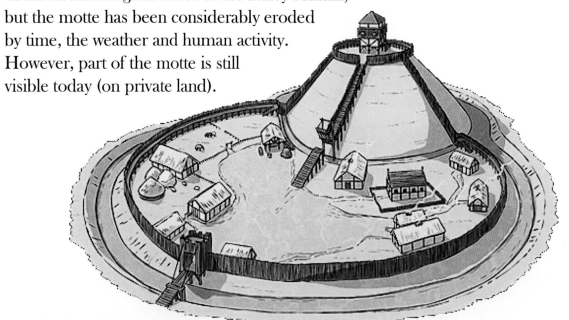

Lorrha's motte and bailey castle might well have looked something like this.

Lorrha Fact Files

ST RUADHÁN'S BELL is cast from copper alloy and dates from the eighth or ninth centuries. It measures 13.8cm high by 8cm wide and was found in the well which provided water for the Augustinian Abbey, before being passed to the British Museum by the 19th century historian and collector T L Cooke in 1854. He had been presented with it some years before by the Reverend Mr O'Brien, Roman Catholic incumbent of Lorrha. In an earlier time, it had been the custom throughout Ireland to swear sacred oaths on named saint's bells.

THE STOWE MISSAL (also known as the Lorrha Missal), is a small Irish illuminated manuscript, hand-written on velum and mainly in Latin, but with some Old Irish included. It originates from the late eighth or early ninth century.

Some pages were rewritten and annotations added at the monastery of St Ruadhán in Lorrha c.AD 1050. The Missal is in the form of a Mass book, which could have been carried by a priest on his travels. About AD 1030 the manuscript was encased within a protective reliquary cover or book-shrine, known as a cumdach. To date, this is one of the oldest found in Ireland. The Missal and its cumdach were found inside a stone wall at Lackeen Castle near Lorrha in the eighteenth century, where they had remained hidden and protected for centuries from Norman and later Protestant attackers, as well as Irish looters.

The Missal was named 'Stowe' because it was discovered in a collection of Irish manuscripts being sold by the Duke of Buckingham of Stowe House, Buckinghamshire, England to the Earl of Ashburnham. In 1883 the British Government purchased it and deposited in the Royal Irish Academy, Dublin. The cumdach is in the care of the National Museum of Ireland, Dublin.

Cape Date and Brandy Tart

Contributed by Stuart, who says:

"The exotic taste of Africa combines with the heady flavour of a good brandy. This makes a fabulously rich dessert!"

INGREDIENTS:

For the tart:

1 cup chopped dates, 1 cup boiling water, 1 tsp bicarbonate of soda

2 tbsp butter	**For the brandy sauce:**
1 cup sugar	2 cups sugar
½ cup walnuts	1 tbsp butter
1 egg	½ cup water
1¼ cups plain flour	1 tsp vanilla extract (or essence)
4 tsp baking powder	½ cup of brandy
Pinch of salt.	

METHOD:

Pre-heat the oven to 160°C / 325°F / Gas mark 3.
23cm / 9-inch circular ovenproof pie dish, well buttered.

Boil the kettle.
In a small bowl, soak the chopped dates in the boiled water with the bicarbonate of soda and allow to cool.

Meanwhile ...

Cream the butter and sugar together very thoroughly.
Add the beaten egg and stir well.
Then add all the other ingredients and combine.
Finally, add the prepared dates in their liquid and mix well.
Pour the mixture into the prepared oven dish and even out the surface.
Bake for approximately ½ hour or until a skewer or cake tester comes out of the middle of the tart clean. Switch the oven off.

Whilst the cooked tart is kept warm in the oven ...

Melt all the sauce ingredients in a pan over a gentle heat.
Remove the tart from the oven, poke a few holes in the surface and pour the sauce all over it.
Return to the oven for a few minutes.
Serve warm. . .
     . . . with cream or custard!

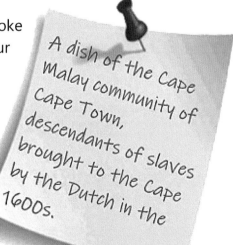

A dish of the Cape Malay community of Cape Town, descendants of slaves brought to the Cape by the Dutch in the 1600s.

The Monastic Village

The monastery established by St Ruadhán is believed to have flourished until the mid-ninth century. During this time it was twice attacked by the Vikings. With the arrival of the Normans in the late twelfth century, the old monastery was re-established, this time as a new priory under the care of the Augustinian Canons and situated within the grounds of the original abbey. This came about as a result of dioscesan reform within Ireland. Bearing these reforms in mind, it is possible to consider the founding of the Augustinian Priory in Lorrha as a continuation of Christian presence in the village, this time following the Rule of St Augustine, rather than the beginning of something completely new. The original, earlier stone church continued to function as the parochial church, with control of the benefice passing to the Augustinians.

The Priory dates from the latter part of the twelfth century, possibly built under the patronage of William de Burgh. During the thirteenth century it was burnt down and rebuilt twice. What remains today dates from the fifteenth century.

The illustration is from a public information panel displayed at the site.

The most imposing reminder of Lorrha's monastic past is the Dominican Friary, the remains of which stand alongside the more recent Roman Catholic Church (built c.1813). The friary was founded in 1269 by Walter de Burgo, Earl of Ulster and 2nd Baron of Connaught and was dedicated to St Peter the Martyr (Peter of Verona). The building was substantial, having a nave and chancel (still to be seen), approximately 46 metres long by 10 metres wide. The lands associated with the friary were considerable, amounting to approximately 54 acres and incorporating the Lorrha River, which powered the flour mills.

The Dominican Order was founded in AD 1215 by St. Dominic. By AD 1300 they had come to Ireland and established 24 friaries, which became centres of worship and learning. The Dominicans were called the "Black Friars" because of their dress.

The friary survived the Dissolution of the Monasteries (AD 1537) and Cromwell's campaign against Ireland. By AD 1688 it had gained considerable importance and continued to function until the very late eighteenth century.

Today, the monument is in the care of the Office of Public Works.

The illustrations are from a public information panel displayed at the site.

Casey's Farm Brown Bread

Contributed by Joan, who says:

"My mother-in-law baked this bread for fifty years. I took it on and have done thirty-five years to date. I hope to continue further and pass it on to my daughter-in-law. It's SO useful..."

INGREDIENTS:

12oz / 340g self-raising flour (sieved)

4oz / 110g plain flour with 1 tsp baking powder
    and ½ tsp bread soda added (sieve this together, too)

4oz / 110g coarse wholemeal flour

½ pint / 285mℓ whole milk and water mixture
    (see METHOD)

Good pinch of salt

METHOD:

Pre-heat the oven to 220°C / 425°F / Gas mark 7.

Place the prepared white flours and raising agents in a bowl and stir to thoroughly combine.
Add the coarse wholemeal flour and stir everything together with a flat, short butter knife. Add the salt.

Add a little warm water to the milk, as milk from the fridge is too cold for the bread to rise well. You should end up with approximately ½ pint / 285mℓ.
Add the milk to the flours and mix well with the short butter knife to combine everything. Your finished dough should not be too wet.

Gather the dough together with your hands, which you have lightly dusted with white flour.
Working quite quickly, shape the dough into a round, place on a baking sheet and pat it down slightly.
Lightly cut a cross across the top of your loaf.

Cook for 15 minutes in the hot oven, then turn the baking tray round and put it back for a further 15 minutes.

Fresh farm brown bread and butter... nothing better!

Enjoy every mouthful...

Chocolate Biscuit Cake

Contributed by Anne Marie.

A touch of luxurious indulgence... especially for the chocoholic! ...

INGREDIENTS:

10oz / 280g crushed digestive biscuits
6oz / 180g butter
6oz / 180g milk chocolate
6oz / 180g 70% cocoa content chocolate
1 large can condensed milk

METHOD:

1 x 15cm / 6-inch tin.
Line your tin with parchment paper.
You will also need a few Kinder Bueno bars, a large bar of Madagascan chocolate and a Cadbury's Curly Wurly bar, and any other decorations.

Melt the butter and both kinds of chocolate from the ingredients list in a pan.
Whip in the condensed milk – work quickly as the mixture thickens within a couple of minutes!

Stir in the crushed digestive biscuits.
Pour the combined mixture into the prepared tin.
Flatten the top.
Cover with a "hat" of parchment paper.

Chill in the fridge until set. For best results, leave overnight.

Gently melt the bar of Madagascan chocolate.
Allow to cool slightly and use to stick the decorations on top of the cake. Use the photograph as an example of the decorated cake.

Cut a slice and enjoy!

Did you know?

Chocolate produces the mood-elevating substance serotonin – also known as the "happiness hormone". Insulin released in response to the sugar allows tryptophan to move to the brain, where it engenders happiness.

Courgette Bread

Contributed by Mary, who says:

"A great recipe to make with a group of children. Lots of jobs: weighing / grating / measuring / beating / chopping / sifting / stirring / greasing. Easy to make — delicious to eat!"

INGREDIENTS:

400g plain flour
½ tsp salt
1 tsp bicarbonate of soda
½ tsp baking powder
1 tsp ground cinnamon
¼ tsp freshly grated nutmeg
¼ tsp ground cloves

300g caster sugar
100g demerara sugar
3 eggs, beaten
200㎖ sunflower oil
2 tsp vanilla extract
380g courgettes, grated with skin left on
75g chopped walnuts

METHOD:

Pre-heat the oven to 150°C / 302°F / Gas Mark 2
Butter or oil and flour 2 x 13cm by 23cm / 5-inch x 9-inch loaf tins

In a large bowl, sift in the flour, salt, bicarbonate of soda, baking powder and spices.
Add both the sugars and stir everything together to mix thoroughly.

Add the beaten eggs, oil, vanilla extract and grated courgettes to the dry ingredients and mix well until combined.
Add the walnuts and fold in gently.
Divide the mixture equally between the two prepared loaf tins.

Bake in the oven for between 1 – 1¼ hours, or until a skewer or cake tester inserted into the middle comes out clean.

Remove from oven and allow to cool in the tins for 20 minutes.
Turn the loaves out onto a wire rack.

Serve slices just as is,
or toast them and add
butter!

Did you know...?
Courgettes contain potassium, Vitamin C and folic acid. Half a courgette is one of your 5-a-day.

More Lorrha Fact Files

MARTIN O'MEARA VC was born at Lissernane, Lorrha, in 1885. He came

from a large family and worked as a woodcutter in southern Ireland before moving to Australia in 1911/1912. He continued working as a wood hewer in Western Australia before joining the Australian Imperial Force (AIF) and serving in World War One. During the Battle of the Somme (1916) he repeatedly rescued wounded from No-Man's-Land and was himself wounded in the process. For his bravery he was awarded the Victoria Cross, the only Australian soldier of Irish descent to do so in that war. He suffered a catastrophic mental collapse upon his return to Australia and spent the rest of his life in psychiatric hospitals. He died in Perth, WA in 1935.

Sketch © 2020 by local artist Ute Rüter-Duggan

ELLA DE BURGH DWYER of Ballyquirk near Lorrha, came from a well-to-do farming family. She inherited over 600 acres and farmed her own land, which was unusual for a gentlewoman of the period. She was highly thought of in the locality generally and by her tenants, to whom she was a generous landlord. In October 1918, during the final weeks of the First World War, she was travelling to England aboard the

RMS Leinster when it was torpedoed in the Irish Sea and sunk. Although a strong swimmer, she did not survive. Her body was recovered and is buried in the Church of Ireland cemetery in Lorrha. Ella was the last of her family line.

MARCH OF O'SULLIVAN-BEARE: Donal Cam O'Sullivan Beare was the last independent ruler of the *Ó Súileabháin Bhéara* family based on the Beara Peninsua in County Cork. At the Battle and Seige of Kinsale (1601-1602) the Irish and allied Spanish forces were defeated by the English. After the fall of Dunboy Castle, Donal Cam gathered about 1,000 of his surviving kin and fled north towards County Leitrim, contending with skirmishes from English and allied Irish forces along the way. The clansmen sought food and shelter in a desolate wintertime amidst a bleak and hostile countryside, but completed this grueling 700 km march in fourteen days. Many left the march en route, including in the Lorrha area. Today, many residents of the parish can trace their ancestry back to these refugees. The march pressed on, crossing the River Shannon, until about 30 survivors finally reached their destination in 1603. The Beara-Breifne Way walking trail follows the line of the historical march, including via Lorrha.

THE STOLEN or VANISHED RAILWAY: In the nineteenth century Ireland was expanding its transport links and by mid-century it was possible to travel from Dublin to Birr. In 1853 it was decided to connect Parsonstown (modern day Birr) to Portumna on the Shannon, thus making it possible to travel from Dublin to Limerick (last stage via the river) and ports further west for access to the Atlantic.

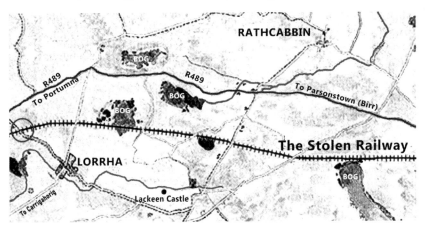

The Parsonstown & Portumna Bridge Railway set about constructing the 12¼ mile line, which finally opened in 1868. Lorrha and Rathcabbin were the two centres of population in the district, but neither was provided with a station stop. Due to spiralling costs, insufficient clientele and an inconvenient timetable, at least from the Parsonstown end, the line closed in 1878. Watchmen over the now silent and deserted line were withdrawn in 1883. Thereafter, the tracks and fittings were "purloined" by the locals and the line gradually "vanished" or was "stolen". What remains of one of the stone bridge supports can still be seen on the approach road to Lorrha village (red circle).

Eilee's Tea Brack

Contributed by Anonymous, who says:

*"...this is a traditional cross between a cake and a bread.
Any number of variations exist, all of which use fruit..."*

INGREDIENTS:

340g / 12oz plain flour
340g / 12oz raisins
225g / 8oz brown sugar
25g / 1oz chopped peel
25g / 1oz glacé cherries

¼ tsp salt
275mℓ / ½ pint good cold tea
1 tsp baking powder
1 egg
¼ tsp mixed spice

METHOD:

Pre-heat the oven to 180°C / 350°F / Gas mark 4.
Butter a 13cm by 23cm / 5-inch x 9-inch loaf tin.

Brew the tea to personal taste regarding strength.
In a large bowl, steep the raisins, chopped peel and cherries with the sugar in the hot tea and leave overnight.
For extra zing, once the tea has cooled, why not add a good slug of whiskey?

In another bowl, sieve together the flour, baking powder, salt and spice then stir well to combine.
Add a little of the flour to the bowl containing the steeped fruit and tea and mix thoroughly.
Add the beaten egg and mix again.
Carefully fold in the remaining flour.

Turn the mixture into the prepared loaf tin and smooth the surface.
Bake for approximately 1 hour.

Test the centre to ensure it's cooked, then remove from the oven.
Allow to cool before turning out from the tin.

When completely cooled, slice and enjoy. A good spread of butter makes it even more delicious. . .

Lorrha's Monasteries Today

Photographs © Roland Dyer

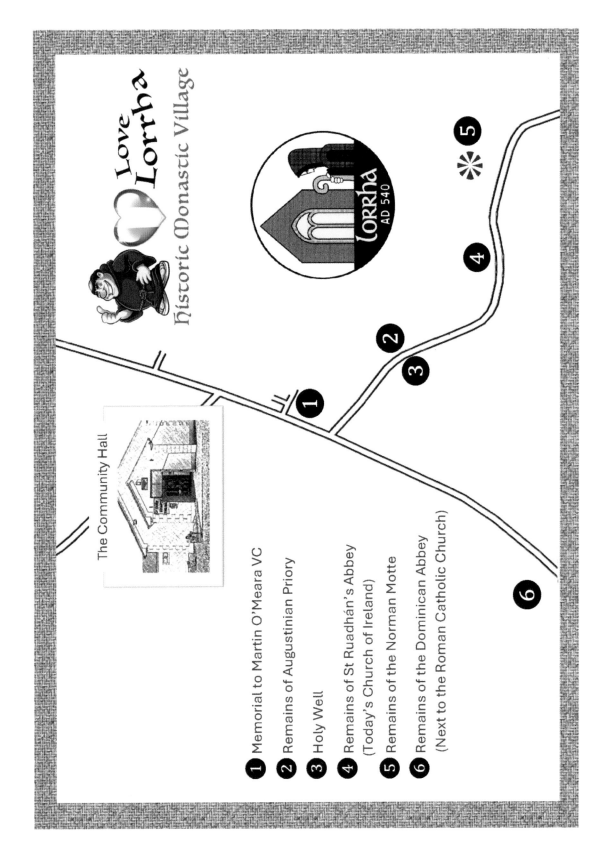

Love Lorrha

Historic Monastic Village

LORRHA AD 540

The Community Hall

1 Memorial to Martin O'Meara VC

2 Remains of Augustinian Priory

3 Holy Well

4 Remains of St Ruadhán's Abbey
(Today's Church of Ireland)

5 Remains of the Norman Motte

6 Remains of the Dominican Abbey
(Next to the Roman Catholic Church)

Eve's Pudding

Contributed by Ann, who says:

"Cooking apples are very plentiful most of the year. This recipe also tastes delicious for dessert with custard or ice cream!"

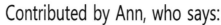

INGREDIENTS:

1 ½ lb / 675g cooking apples
4oz / 110g demerara sugar
4oz / 110g butter
4oz / 110g caster sugar
2 eggs
5oz / 140g self-raising flour
½ tsp vanilla essence
Flaked almonds
Grated zest of 1 large lemon

Quick tip:
Try to grate only the zest of the lemon. Avoid the white pith, which can be bitter.

METHOD:

Pre-heat the oven to 180˚C / 350˚F / Gas mark 4.
Ovenproof dish, buttered.

Meanwhile . . .

Peel, core and slice the apples thinly.
Arrange the slices in the buttered overproof dish.
Sprinkle with the demerara sugar, the grated lemon rind and
1 tablespoon (15mℓ) of cold water.

Cream together butter and caster sugar until light and fluffy.
Whisk the egg and the vanilla essence.
Beat this into the creamed mixture a little at a time.

Sift the flour and fold it into the creamed mixture a little at a time, with
a metal spoon.
When completely combined, carefully spoon the mixture evenly over
the apples in the buttered dish.
Sprinkled a good handful of flaked almonds on the top.

Bake in the oven for 35 - 40 minutes, or until a skewer comes out clean.

Now the hard part – serve it with custard or cream?

Fresh Fruit Pavlova

Contributed by Nancy, who says:

"This is my recipe. Others might have their own variations."

INGREDIENTS:

For the MERINGUE:
6 large fresh eggs (whites only to be used - must be at room temperature)
330g caster sugar
1 or 2 teaspoons Gem (gluten-free) cornflour
1 teaspoon white wine vinegar
Vanilla extract (**or** vanilla essence)
Lemon juice

For the FILLING:
500mℓ fresh cream
3 tablespoons crème fraiche
1 teaspoon caster sugar
Selection of fresh fruit (strawberries, black & white grapes, blueberries, Kiwi fruit and banana)

METHOD:

Preheat oven to 150°C / 130°C fan / 300°F / Gas Mark 2.
A baking sheet and non-stick parchment paper (I use a pizza tray).

Weigh the sugar into a glass bowl. Warm in the oven for approximately 10 minutes. Warmed sugar dissolves faster when mixed with the egg whites.

Make sure your mixing bowl is clean and dry – wipe it with lemon juice and dry thoroughly before use.
Separate the egg whites from the yolks (use the yolks to make custard – I use them when making a quiche).
Put egg whites into your mixing bowl and whisk at medium speed until they form stiff peaks and are glossy (don't over-whisk!). Add a spoon of the warmed sugar at a time and whisk well after each addition until all sugar is used (this may take over a quarter to a half hour). Add the cornflour, a few drops of lemon juice and the vanilla extract to the mixture and whisk. Check if the sugar is completely dissolved by rubbing a little of the mixture between your fingers. If it feels gritty, it needs extra beating.

In the meantime, line your baking tray with the parchment paper. Dab the meringue mixture in the corners of the baking tray to stick the parchment paper in position. I suggest drawing a 9-inch circle on the paper.

Once the mixture is ready, spoon it onto the tray within the circle and heap it high. Turn the oven down to 130°C / 110°C fan / 265°F / 230 °F fan / Gas Mark 1. Place the tray on the middle shelf of the oven. After half an hour turn the oven down to 100°C / 80°C fan / 210°F / 175° F fan / Gas Mark ¼. Cook for a further hour and a half. Once cooked, turn off the oven and let the meringue cool off in the oven with the door closed, preferably overnight.

Whisk the cream, sugar and crème fraiche together to form soft peaks. Spoon the mixture over the meringue, then arrange the fruit on top.

Enjoy a slice as 1 of your 5-a-day!

Fruit Slices

Contributed by Marian.

Dried fruit of various kinds always add a touch of the exotic, not to mention sweetness, to any baking. These Fruit Slices are no exception.

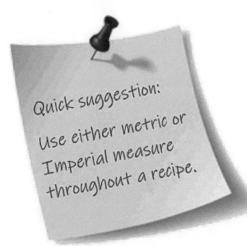

Quick suggestion:
Use either metric or Imperial measure throughout a recipe.

INGREDIENTS:

1lb / 450g mixed dried fruit
1 tub of cherries, chopped
12oz / 340g caster sugar
2 tsp almond essence
3 eggs
8oz / 225g butter or margarine
12oz / 340g plain flour
2 tsp baking powder

METHOD:

Pre-heat the oven to 160°C / 325°F / Gas mark 3.
1 roasting tin, 20cm x 30cm / 8-inch x 12-inch, greased.

Place the fruit in a saucepan and cover with water.
Bring to the boil, then simmer for 5 minutes.
Turn off the heat and leave to cool.

When saucepan contents are cold, drain off the liquid and leave the fruit in the saucepan.
Add the butter to the fruit and melt over a low heat.
Remove from the heat and allow to cool.

Mix the sugar, almond essence and eggs.
Add the egg mixture to the cold fruit and butter mixture and combine thoroughly.
Finally, add the flour and baking powder and mix well.

Pour the mixture into the prepared tin and smooth out evenly.

Bake for approximately 1¼ hours.

Cut into good size slices and enjoy! ...

Even More Lorrha Fact Files

SERGEANT PHILIP BRADY: Irish history is complex, often violent and frequently bloody. Even a small village such as Lorrha experienced its share of upheaval and turbulence, be it at the hands of the Vikings, the Normans, internal struggles between Irish local chiefs or English invaders.

Sergeant Brady of the Royal Irish Constabulary had been in post in Lorrha for less than a week when he, together with two other constables, set out on patrol down the road to Carrigahorig. The night of 2nd September, 1919 was clear and moonlit. On the return journey, the patrol was about half a mile from Lorrha when two shots rang out, hitting the sergeant and one of the constables. Brady had become yet another fatality in the War of Independence (1919-1921), a struggle that was to continue until the signing of the Anglo-Irish Treaty in December, 1921. This did not bring peace to Ireland, but led to a Civil War (1922-1923) between pro and anti-Treaty factions.

Another military figure from Lorrha was **FELIX JOSEPH CRONIN,** who fought through both the wars mentioned above and rose to the rank of Quartermaster General of the Irish National Army. The Cronin family was well known in Lorrha and the wider parish, several generations of whom taught at the local national school.

THE BURNING OF PORTLAND PARK HOUSE: Located a few miles outside of Lorrha, Portland Park House was a fine example of late Georgian archectiture dating from the 1820s. It was owned by the Butler-Stoney family, major land owners in Tipperary, but had stood unoccupied for almost a decade, being maintained by 3 servants. Major Butler-Stoney eventually handed the house over to the trustees of Emmanuel Home of Dublin as a refuge for Protestant children. Some members of the local community did not want this and took the law into their own hands. During the early hours of Tuesday, May 10th, 1938 the house was burned to the ground. Fortunately, there were no injuries.

ETHEL SARA STONEY: The Stoneys were a Protestant Anglo-Irish gentry family from both County Tipperary and County Longford. Ethel herself was born in India before being sent back to Ireland for her education and then to England to "remove her brogue". She was a descendant of George Stoney (1713-1787) of Portland Park House, Lorrha parish. In 1907, she married J.M. Turing, an official of the Indian Civil Service, and they had two sons. Several of Ethel's family members excelled in the fields of science, mathematics, physics, medicine and engineering, genes which their youngest son must have inherited from his mother. Alan Turing, regarded by many as the father of artificial intelligence (AI) and theoretical computer science, was one of the leading codebreakers at Bletchley Park during World War

II. He was also instrumental in the development of morphogenesis, the identification of patterns and shapes in biological organisms.

THE GAELIC ATHLETICS ASSOCIATION was founded in 1884 in Thurles, Co. Tipperary, as a national organisation to make traditional Irish cultural sports accessible to the masses through clubs established throughout the country. Lorrha-Dorrha GAA was founded in 1885 and devloped a reputation in the sport of hurling. The club moved through several homes until the present one was established and named, appropriately, St Ruadhán's Park. The purpose-built facilities comprise 3 playing fields, a clubhouse with four dressing rooms, a sports hall and gym.

Over the years the club has included many notable hurlers, perhaps the most famous being Tony Reddin (1919-2015), regarded as hurling's greatest ever goalkeeper. In honour of his achievements and to his memory, the club's home was renamed Tony Reddin Park and Community Centre in 2019.

Granny's Fruit Cake

Contributed by Catherine, who remembers:

"This is a very light fruit cake. My Granny, Maureen Sullivan Moatfield, always used to say it was her 'I pot Wonder!'"

Quick tip:
Measure all your ingredients using the same size mug or cup...

INGREDIENTS:

½ lb / 227g Stork margarine
A mug of water
A mug of sugar
300g sultanas
(or fruit of your choice)
1 tsp of mixed spice
1 tsp of ground cinnamon
4 eggs
2 mugs of flour

METHOD:

Pre-heat your oven to 150°C / 302°F / Gas mark 2.

Place the Stork margarine, water, sugar and fruit in a pan.
Bring to the boil and then simmer gently for about 15 minutes.
Allow to cool.

When cool, add the mixed spice, cinnamon, eggs and flour.
Mix well, until everything is combined.
Divide the mixture into 2 x 1lb greased and lined loaf tins.
Alternatively, you can use a single 2lb tin, prepared in the same way
as before. Use greaseproof paper for lining.

When the correct oven temperature is reached, put your cake in and
bake for 90 minutes.
When cooked, place on a wire tray and allow to cool a little in the tin.
Then turn out from the tin onto your wire cooling rack.

Serving suggestion:
Remove the greaseproof paper and cut your baked cake into slices.

It will taste even better with a little spread of butter. . .

Harriet's Apple Cake

Contributed by David, who remembers:

"This recipe was my Aunt's 'special treat' cake. She always put a single glacé cherry in the mix and, as children, whoever found it in their slice felt they were really the lucky one!"

INGREDIENTS:

140g / 5oz caster sugar

110g / 4oz self-raising flour

110g / 4oz ground almonds

140g / 5oz butter

1 whole glacé cherry (most important!)

3 hen's eggs or 2 duck eggs, beaten

2 good cooking apples

1 tsp baking powder

A good handful of flaked almonds

METHOD:

Pre-heat the oven to 140°C / 275°F / Gas mark 1.
You need 1 x 20cm / 8-inch springform loose bottom cake tin.
Butter and then flour the sides well, shaking out any excess flour.
Line the base of the tin with a circle of greaseproof paper to fit.
Cut a second circle same size as above and cut out a 4-inch diameter hole in the middle. Put aside until later.

Peel and core the apples, then cut into slices or bite-sized chunks.

Mix the sugar, flour, ground almonds and baking powder together thoroughly in a bowl. Next, melt the butter.
Separately, beat the eggs well. Add the melted butter and beaten eggs to the dry ingredients and mix very thoroughly.

Take the cake tin and put approximately one third of the mixture into it.
Next, arrange a layer of the apple pieces on top of the batter in the tin.
Add the single glacé cherry and then spread the remainder of the batter mixture over the apple pieces or slices (and the cherry!).
Finally, sprinkle flaked almonds over the top of the cake.

Bake in the over for approximately 50 minutes.

Then lay the second sheet of greaseproof paper (with the hole cut into it) over the top of the partially baked cake. Return to oven for a further 20 minutes, or until a cake tester or skewer inserted in the middle comes out clean. I find that this stops the middle of the cake sinking!

Remove baked cake from the springform tin and allow to cool.
This cake makes a delicious dessert when served with cream, Greek yoghurt or mascarpone.

Mammy's Christmas Pudding

Contributed by Carmel, who says:

"Mammy always made Christmas puddings as family presents. When she passed away, I kept up the tradition and have added my own secret ingredient!"

<u>INGREDIENTS</u> (makes 2 puddings):

180g / 6oz self-raising flour	1 tub mixed peel
1 level tsp mixed spice	1 tub glacé cherries (halved)
1 level tsp ground cinnamon	50g / 2oz chopped almonds
½ level tsp ground nutmeg	Grated zest of 1 orange and 1 lemon
225g / 8oz white breadcrumbs	225g / 8oz margarine
340g / 12oz dark brown sugar	3 large eggs
225g / 8oz raisins	1 tbsp **each** of brandy, whiskey and
225g / 8oz sultanas	Jägermeister
450g / 1lb currants	275mℓ / ½ pint Guinness

METHOD:

2 x 1 litre pudding bowls with tight fitting lids. Bowls well-greased.
2 x circles of greaseproof paper for top of the bowls

Melt the margarine and allow to cool slightly.
Sieve the flour and spices into a large bowl, then add the breadcrumbs, sugar, fruit, nuts, lemon and orange zests.
Mix thoroughly and then make a well in the centre.

In another bowl, beat the eggs, then add the Guinness and cooled margarine. Mix well.
Add this egg mixture to the dry ingredients.

Next, add the whiskey, brandy and Jägermeister.
Cover the bowl with a damp tea towel and allow to stand overnight. The mixture is very wet at this stage but will soak up overnight.

Next day, mix very well using a wooden spoon.
Distribute the mixture equally between the two pudding bowls.
Place a greaseproof circle on the top of each pudding mixture.
Cover each bowl with its tight-fitting lid.

Put a saucer or small flat plate in the bottom of a deep saucepan.
Place a pudding bowl on top.
Half-fill the saucepan with boiling water, then cover the pan with a tightly fitting lid. Boil for 6 hours, topping up with boiling water from time to time.

Before serving, reheat by boiling again for 1 hour.

Shauna's Carrot Cake

Contributed by Una, who says:

"This is a very simple cake to make, but oh so delicious ! Thoroughly recommended !"

INGREDIENTS:

250g / 9oz plain flour
2 tsp bread soda
½ tsp fine sea salt
1 ½ tsp ground cinnamon
295mℓ / ½ pint vegetable oil
400g / 14oz light soft
   brown sugar
1 tsp vanilla extract
4 large eggs
300g grated carrots
100g / 4oz chopped pecans
65g / 2 ½ oz raisins

For the filling:
225g / 8oz cream cheese
140g / 5oz icing sugar
80mℓ / 6 tbsp double cream
For decoration:
Handful of whole pecans

METHOD:

Pre-heat the oven to 180˚C / 350˚F / Gas mark 4.
2 x 23cm / 9-inch round cake pans, buttered and lined.

To make the batter for the cake:
Mix all the dry ingredients in one bowl until well blended.
Whisk all the wet ingredients together in another bowl.

Switch to a rubber spatula and fold the wet and dry ingredients together until no flour streaks are observed!

Add the grated carrots, raisins and pecans to the batter.
Divide the batter between the two buttered and lined round pans.
Bake in a pre-heated oven for 35-45 mins.

To make the frosting:
Incorporate the cream cheese and icing sugar with a hand-held mixer then beat in the cream for 1 minute.
Chill in the fridge until required.

After baking, let the two cakes cool on wire racks.
When cool, frost one cake and place the second layer on top.
With the remaining filling, frost the top of the cake.
Decorate with additional whole pecans.

Relax and enjoy a good size slice... or two!

Acknowledgements

Cover, layout, text and research	Stuart Fifield
Photography	Roland Dyer
Production Assistants	Pauline Abbott, Barbara Tierney
Wooden Bread Boards	David Sullivan

Contributors

	Anonymous
Joan	Casey
Mary	Coen
Suzanne	Corcoran
Ann	Coughlan
Una	Dempsey
Stuart	Fifield
David	Hewitt
Anne Marie	Hough
Marian	Quirke
Catherine	Raleigh
Ute	Rüter-Duggan
Carmel	Slevin
Nancy	White

In addition to the talented people listed above, this north Tipperary parish is home to individuals who possess expertise in many fields including: baking, basket weaving, beekeeping, hairdressing, jam making, jewellery designing, knitting, landscape gardening, market gardening and woodworking. The parish also lists artists, a blacksmith, farmers (cattle, goats, sheep and tillage), a graphic artist, historians, an IT specialist, a nurseryman, an acclaimed photographer, a playwright, publicans, sportsmen, sportswomen, storytellers and writers amongst its numbers. These combined skills and talents go towards making the fabric of the community what it is today.

Printed in Great Britain
by Amazon

AUTHOR'S NOTE

WARNING

This book is not suitable for children, people of a nervous disposition, or people who are easily offended by ideologically sensitive topics as this story contains dark and suggestive themes, mild language, graphic violence and gore in both text and illustrated form which some readers may find disturbing. Reader discretion is advised.

http://farumir.deviantart.com/

https://www.facebook.com/francine.woodward

http://farumirworks.daportfolio.com/

FARUMIR Works

THE CIRCUS WOLFMAN

Written and illustrated by

Francine Woodward

In memory of Malcolm Pape

"A truly great man and a loving Grandfather
who saw the good in everyone."

1925 - 2013

"A Circus is a prison, it even looks the same…a Circus is a prison; but it has another name."

– The Joey in Yoram Gross' Dot around the World.

ACT I

The circus; a place in your childhood that brings you joy and fun filled entertainment, where you laugh at the dancing clowns and gasp in awe at the daring acrobats. As a child you dream of being in a circus as the star of the show. As an adult you bring your own children to the circus to share with them the same admiration for the performance from your memories. So innocent, so happy…so ignorant. And naïve to believe that a circus is a dreamy career and a wonderful way to live. Well forgive me for not being sorry to tell you the harsh truth. To tell you that your childish perception of life in a circus is incorrect and utterly so. Whether you want to believe it or not, it is true nonetheless that being in a circus is like being in jail; you have no freedom, no privacy or privileges, and once you are in the troupe you die in it because you can never leave. Far behind the colourful spotlights and sawdust ring is the real face of the circus that everyone ignores in favour of the less depressing and more appealing mask. You are probably sceptical of this fact, but how would you know any facts at all if you have never been in a troupe? The answer is simple; you wouldn't. But I do, because I am. So before you judge and shun the shattering of the delusion from your youth; sit back on your soft cushioned chair and listen as the secrets of the circus are told straight from the horse's mouth…or should I say the wolf's mouth?

It is common knowledge that half of a circus' acts are heavily reliant on animals and not just any animals, but large and exotic animals; the bigger the better, and the prettier or scarier the creature, the louder the crowd cheers. Dancing bears, marching elephants, juggling seals and tamed lions, they are exciting to see. For some reason.

Some circuses also have what you call 'Freak Shows'. The clue to what that is exactly is in the name. A collection of rare oddities that defy nature, from bearded women and grown men smaller than toddlers, to women with male organs and men with swollen tumours all over their faces. People who are greatly different from the norm displayed in chains to the public for money and labelled 'freaks'. That is exactly what I am. I am a freak. I am also an animal too, the rarest and scariest animal of all. I am the main star of Circus Grimm's freak show.

Circus Grimm is a travelling circus troupe that lives up to its name for everything about it is grim…but that is not what makes Circus Grimm the most popular circus of its time. This circus' freak show does not just focus on human freaks you see; they showcase monsters. Real monsters. Their biggest monster out of all the freaks is a creature that has crossed the boundary between man and beast, an unnatural hybrid of blood that should never mix; they call me the 'Circus Wolfman'. Because that is what I am. I am a werewolf, a true freak of nature, and you don't get any rarer and scarier than that.

Circus Grimm made its reputation by collecting the most bizarre and terrifying of freaks; reptilian men, three headed anacondas, pig-faced witches, giantesses – I can go on and on but I do not wish to bore you with too many irrelevant details. However, the circus' greatest achievement was the obtaining and containing of sufferers of lycanthropy. Real lycanthropy, not just some poor soul with a personality disorder or just abnormal hair-growth; I'm talking about the real thing of countless legends around the world. Creatures that are half human and half wolf, but you probably already know what a lycanthrope is. Just in case you don't know it's just the fancy name for werewolf. No other circus in the country, or even the whole world, has ever had such vicious beasts held captive on stage for all to see. And with good reason…werewolves are not trainable dogs, we can never be tamed, and we never trust or serve. Other circuses know this, but Circus Grimm doesn't care, they just want fame and fortune. Little do they know though, that such recklessness spawned from greed will be the death of them someday, and I hope that I will be their death, or at least be there to watch it die…

I was not the first werewolf ever featured in the Freak show; I am the third. The first werewolf was too old to keep the crowds amused so they replaced it with a new werewolf, but that wolf too had a short career, as it died of a heart-attack caused by its great fear of fire when they tried to get it to jump through a burning hoop. And so here I am, still alive and still knocking the crowd dead (oh how I wish I could do that literally). Miserable I gaze through the bars of my cage, resigned to this wretched life in the grip of a cruel fate. Reduced from a feared beast of nightmares to an enslaved plaything for gawking idiots who deliberately turn their backs on our suffering. I am no more than a spectacle for my captors to torment and abuse. Loneliness rules my life as I look on at the world beyond my prison, watching the process of time fly by me and I can only dream of the freedom my heart longs for. I can't remember the last time I felt grass under my feet; I have been stuck in a rusty cage behind faded curtains for so long that my fur has turned black from the seclusion of the sun. I have contemplated suicide a fair number of times…but for some reason something always holds me back from just either starving myself or taking my claws and slitting my own throat with them. Damn survival instincts.

I huff and sigh, my hot breath making white clouds in the freezing air. My fur and fat keep me warm but I still feel cold, and these thin rags for blankets and all this damp hay covering the cage's floor does very little to help. I hear the circus folks shouting and moving around; they are preparing for tonight's show and getting ready to let the audience into the seating. I hear the usual voices shout *'Roll up! Roll up! Step right up to the Freak Show! Come see the Circus Wolfmen!'* And I groan in annoyance. That's my cue, time to start faking savagery and falsifying fervour to get the audience going. Before my outbursts of violence and ferocity were sincere…now it is all just an act.

They don't clap or cheer if you don't do anything scary enough. If I don't get enough screams from people then I get whipped, but if I get too many screams that make them run away I get whipped again. I just can't win. There is no pleasing anyone in show business, take it from me. Actually, I don't really need to do much to frighten customers – just seeing my bared fangs the size of kitchen knives and my huge talons curved like butcher's meat-hooks is enough to make even the bravest of men shudder. But for what any of it is worth, expressing just how much I want to chew their faces off then pick my teeth with their rib bones is a decent stress relief. The smell of their fear is just so intoxicating…it's like smelling freshly baked cookies on a summer afternoon; tempting and delicious.

But the only fools I can never seem to scare are the clowns. Oh god those damn clowns…I hate them, I hate them all! They know I'm trapped, they know that as long as they don't come too close to the bars I can't do a thing to them, and they use that to their advantage whenever they can to get their laughs. They're as miserable as me, so miserable that they need to take out their frustration on others who are even more miserable than them just to make themselves feel better. They don't get paid enough nor treated well enough, so they vent out their bitter discontentment on the freaks. They'll throw food at the giantesses to mock their grotesque obesity, they'll mug the dwarves knowing that they are too short to take back their stolen belongings from the much taller clowns. The clowns will even go as far as to harass the poor women of the freak show like groping the chest of the three-breasted lady, and stripping the hermaphrodite of all lower garments to humiliate her…doing such ghastly things that make rats look like princes in comparison make my fur bristle and my nose wrinkle in total disgust. They would lose those dirty hands to my jaws if not for these cursed bars and chains binding me.

But I am their favourite target. The audience want to see captive werewolves more than they want to see the clowns and the clowns don't like that one little bit. They get jealous of the better acts very easily, especially me, and they respond to the object of their jealousy with petty bullying.

Here they come now, speak of the devil, and right on schedule; they always visit my cage before I am fed, every time without fail. They taunt me with humourless puns about wolves and dogs, tease me with food that they never give me, but what really irks me is when they start mocking my life. When they joke about my imprisonment, talk about how ugly and hated I am…in other words when they laugh at me for being a werewolf behind bars. I lunge at them when they do, startling them but only for a moment, then they laugh louder at my pointless attempt to break free and savage them.

But even though I know myself that it's pointless, I still snarl at them and shake the bars as hard as I can in a useless effort to snap them in half. I actually managed to once, but that was a mistake on my behalf. I should've done it at night whilst everyone was asleep and the guards were away; I shouldn't have broken the bars in full view of everyone while still on the trailer behind the moving wagon. I didn't get enough time to make a run for it before I was clubbed behind the skull then pinned down while dazed. So now my new bars are made of denser, heavier metal and reinforced with concrete, and the gaps in between the bars made smaller. It's impossible to break these horrible bars a second time now. I mentally kick myself for not planning my breakout properly, but it was the bloody clowns fault; they make me so angry that I can't think straight.

Quickly I tire myself out and slump down in a corner of the cage. The clowns also grow tired and leave, chuckling. I keep my hard glare fixed on them until they are out of sight. They treat me like a toothless mutt, forgetting that half of me is human (or they don't care). They don't realise that their death sits in this cage and I remember every little thing they do and say to me. This cage won't protect them from my big sharp teeth forever – one of these days they'll slip up and get too close and then I really WILL kill them. I'll kill them all, and I will relish it. I SWEAR it. They think all they're doing is clowning around. It's never clever to clown around with a werewolf, even if it's caged. If you do then you are clowning around with death…because an animal never forgets, and a human never forgives.

The animal keeper is coming now. I can hear his soggy footsteps as he treads through the muddy straw, and I can smell the fodder he's brought for us in a rusty bucket. The animals suddenly start going wild in their confinements, shrieking loudly with hunger like monkeys in a zoo (then again a circus IS a zoo in a way). When they hear the keeper coming and see him carrying bags and buckets, they know that it means it's time to eat.

He starts chucking lumps of mushy animal-feed to the calmer of the animals first, then handing out packaged meals to the human freaks next. He leaves the dangerous animals and inhuman freaks until last, since they cause the most trouble during feeding time.

He very cautiously and slowly opens the cage door a little, while another keeper distracts the prisoners with a stick, and quietly fills their food bowls, then quickly pulls his hand away and practically slams the door shut again and locks it immediately. Just in time before the monstrous creatures can make a rapid move for his delicious-looking arm.

My mouth is already watering as he finally comes to my cage. He doesn't seem to mind me though, because he knows I'm different from the others: he knows that I will not attack him. He looks at me, his eyes asking for permission to enter my jail; I silently stare at him for a bit before backing away from the door to let him in. He sighs in relief and opens the door but remains just as cautious with me as he does with the other wolves. He doesn't usually have trouble with me but he still doesn't trust me. He shouldn't either because he lost three of his right hand's fingers to me the first time we met.

I attacked him a number of times when I was new to the circus, but not now; I've learned that he's just a feeder. And while I would much prefer to eat him rather than the smelly portions of meaty slop he gives, I don't want to get clubbed or stabbed in the face by the baton or cattle-prod that all the keepers carry for protection. They're not silver but they still hurt an awful lot. Besides, he's one of the rare few people here who doesn't toy with me. Sure, he's slyly stroked my tail when I wasn't looking once or twice, but something like that is not something I mind. Much.

The keepers try their best to ration out the food evenly between us all, but when some animals and freaks require larger portions than others it's not easy. The Circus 'stars', however, always get the biggest portions, regardless of who needs them most. I'm the Lead Act of the freak show so I get the biggest and freshest shank of meat.

I just look at it. I'm hungry and I know it's mine to eat, but I don't want to eat it. I don't understand it myself, but for some reason meat from prey that wasn't killed by me just doesn't look appetising. Must be a predator thing; maybe that's why the playing dead trick works every time.

I poke and prod the juicy flayed limb of what smells like sheep or goat with my claw, as if I'm unconsciously trying to stir any signs of life from it. Eventually I give in to hunger and lean over to give it a few licks, before chewing through some of the butchered leg to expose the bloodied white bone. But my chewing is sluggish and my stomach churns a little as if it's agreeing that someone else's kill is not a worthy meal. Like the old saying goes; you can lead a horse to water but you can't make it drink it.

I sit back again and whine quietly to myself. I miss killing. That sounds morbid and sadistic I know, but you would never understand if you've never hunted. If you're as vegetarian as a rabbit. When you are a carnivore, a predator, there is something very satisfying about a successful catch. The thrill of the chase alone makes you feel so alive and free, and catching your prize gives you a sense of pride. To know that you have become in charge of another life's fate is so empowering. It's wonderful. People say it's evil, but how is it? To eat what you kill yourself is natural and, if anything, much more respectful to the prey than it is to mutilate its corpse, then give it away. I find it insulting to both the prey and the predator when somebody kills not for food but for sport. Why use only the head and skin, then throw away the rest? What a meaningless waste! Don't you learn in church that it's a sin to waste food?

A loud ruckus diverts my attention away from my unfinished meal. I look over to a larger cage next to me. The source of the noisy disturbance is coming from my fellow werewolves who are all 'arguing' viciously with each over. Wondering why I'm not kept in the same cage as them? I can't answer that because I honestly don't know either. Maybe it's because I'm everybody's favourite freak. But if that's the case then I'd hate to imagine myself being the most disliked freak around here, if this is the way they treat 'favourites'. The most probable reason might be the fact that I'm the most unpredictable of the wolves; the keepers probably don't trust me around other freaks or animals. Maybe they're right; maybe I would turn on whatever poor creature was unfortunate enough to share my prison with me. I'd most likely rip their face off just for so much as making too much noise around me, just because I can.

Speaking of noise, my neighbours are turning more violent as they each try to grab the best meat before it's all gone. I watch them from my cage, my brethren, fighting over their share of food like starved feral dogs. Their barks and yelps earn a suppressed growl from me. Half of me wants to join in while the other half wishes for them to just shut up and kill each other.

It is not just the cages that separate us. I am not like them, we are not a pack; there are no Alphas or Omegas here. We are nothing more than circus freaks and I am the star attraction...they are just the sideshow.

ACT II

Just a few hours before the show we are fed, but they slip drugs into our swill to make us weak and docile. It is so that they can get us out of our cages easier, since the poison hidden in our food makes it next to impossible to struggle. But of course they do not drug us too late before the show, otherwise we cannot perform. They do it hours in advance so that, by the time the medicine's effects have worn off, we are already out of our cells and prepared backstage (still bound by tight iron handcuffs, steel muzzles and chain leashes of course, just until the curtains open). The other beasts fight with all they have, stupidly. But not me. I did in the past but I have learned that resistance is futile… so I reluctantly accept the hardships of my slavery, because what other choice do I have?

They lead me into the ring by a chain leash while the lights dim dark enough to conceal my entrance from the silent audience. While everyone's quiet and the lights are dimmed, the keepers quickly and skilfully remove my muzzle and unclasp the leash from around my neck and wrists. They use cattle prods to stop me from turning on them and special arm-long poles with hooks to carefully free my mouth and paws without risking getting bitten or scratched. Again I no longer bother attempting such assaults on the keepers, but they still take no chances with the strongest and most unpredictable freak in the Circus. I have proven to them that my intelligence is matched only by my strength and 'popularity' with the audience. If I was a free wolf and in a real pack I would very easily rise to the rank of Alpha and the Ringmaster is aware of this, so I always receive harsher 'training' than the other werewolves do; he tries his best to make me submissive, to make sure that I can be controlled. I regret to say that his method works, and what's worse is that my obedience makes the other werewolves obedient as well. That actually makes sense if you know how werewolves operate. Werewolf packs' hierarchy is anarchy; the smartest, strongest werewolf leads and the others follow. So if you control the alpha…you control the whole pack.

Suddenly I am blinded by a big flash of light beaming down on me. The spotlight is on and the audience clap loudly. Once my vision returns I see the hoops and stools are already set up before me. The sound of a cracking whip startles me and I turn to snarl at the whipper behind me, but he cracks his whip again, only this time he aims for my face. I reflectively recoil backwards with a shrill yelp as the tips of the whip's forks just catch the tip of my nose. He won't tolerate any 'back-talk' from me. I snort like an angry bull then turn back around and jump onto the first stool. The first thing I do before starting my act is make myself look as big as possible, then roar louder than a lion, finishing it with a long, petrifying howl. The audience love it. I don't though – it makes my throat sore after a while, and a werewolf with a lost voice is hardly intimidating.

The whip cracks the air once more, giving me the signal to begin the act. The hoop is set on fire and the 'tamer' on the other side of it is ready with his chair and cane. A guttural growl rumbles in my chest as I leap forward. It's show time.

Each and every performance is torture, and the Circus performs from dawn 'til dusk every day, anywhere they can. I am forced to either play the tame trained monkey for the crowd, or be punished by both the staff and the audience for refusing to act out the role I'm given. One time I was whipped so hard and so many times that I passed out, and if it's not whips punishing me, it's mushy tomatoes and sometimes the occasional liquor bottle (one hit me right in the eye once and I was blinded in that eye for the rest of the night). And from the amount of times I've literally had egg all over my face for missing a hoop, I could make the world's biggest omelette.

So I carry out every task I'm burdened with to the very best of my capability. Chasing clowns, 'fighting' tamers, jumping through burning hoops, letting people stick their arms or heads between your jaws yet not allowing you to bite down…I think that's probably the hardest job for me and the other animals to do – having food right there resting on your tongue, teasing your hunger the same way a bully would tease a puppy with biscuits. I hate all of those jobs with a burning passion hotter than the hoops' flames. But what can I do? I'm just a freak of nature, and apparently freaks have no say in anything; circus freaks have no rights.

Can you imagine what it feels like to be licked by flames, pelted by rotten fruit and eggs, hit with chairs, stabbed with canes and struck with whips endlessly? When the ignorant audience leave and the curtains close, the nights are no kinder. Imprisoning bars cage my mind as well as flesh; every night I am tormented by echoes of the circus' cruel cheers and heckles, and my sanity ripped apart by the voices of my memories. The same deathly eyes and bloodied faces of my sinful past haunt me and blame me. They ask me the same horrible questions that I can never answer like *'why did you kill me?'* and *'why did you take away my friends and family?'* continuously. *It wasn't my fault...I can't help it...I'm cursed...I tried to stop myself...I'm sorry...leave me alone...*I beg for forgiveness over and over as I instinctively try to shield my ears from the voices in my head, but ghosts are deaf to pleading and excuses. My only pillow is almost a sponge now with my tears; monsters can cry too you know.

I've forgotten how I became this ungodly creature. I cannot recall how long I have been subjected to this purgatory. I can't even remember how I became a part of this nightmarish freak show in the first place...so I guess it's true what they say: in Hell, time stops.

Full moon shows are the worst. What is supposed to be a night of freedom for my kind is instead a night of suffering for us. Rather than feeling excitement we feel nothing but dread; as the moon grows fatter, so too grows our despair. For them the approaching full moon means profit. Tickets sell out instantly at this time of the month, no matter where the circus goes. Their greedy eyes see only money.

Three days before the full moon they start giving us much less food than usual; just enough to keep us alive but not enough to satisfy us, and then on the last day before the full moon they starve us. On the night when the moon is at its fullest and highest, they throw two of us at a time into the ring with a tall cage installed to prevent any attempts at escape. The moon's power makes us mad, hunger makes us madder. Fuelled with adrenalin and driven insane from starvation, savage instincts take over with maximum force. We go at each other with everything we've got, not caring about the other's life. The only thing on our minds during the fight is food. We've learned that we only get fed after the show, so we want to end the fight as soon as possible. The only way to end the fight is to win, so we each desperately attack our chosen opponents of the night in the hopes of receiving the feast awaiting the survivors.

It doesn't help that we're all 'mongrels', and by that I mean we were all once people; none of us here were born werewolves, we were either bitten by a werewolf or cursed by gypsies or witches. Those who are born with this curse grow up with it and learn to live with it; they even learn how to control it. Since wolf's blood has run through their veins since their birth the wolf's instincts come naturally to them. But us 'mongrels' are different from the pure-bloods; we were born human so when we are cursed our bodies do not know how to cope with this new foreign blood rushing through us. We cannot truly adapt to the changes…so when the full moon transforms us, we don't know how to act. So when it comes to interacting with other werewolves when you're not a pure-blood werewolf, the ending results vary…but here in Circus Grimm where we are 'bred' and trained to fight, killing each other is all we know and all we can do.

While I can't remember how I came to be what I am now, I do know that a majority of the other werewolves here were bought and paid for from shady hunters with less than respectable reputations looking to make easy money. Some of these poor bastards were actually just thieves and beggars who the Circus' night watchmen caught stealing supplies and money or sleeping in the carts…it was the Ringmaster's cruel idea of a punishment and a means of cutting corners at the same time. The robbers and vagrants get taught a horrible lesson, and the Circus gets some new werewolves for the Freak Show without spending a single penny…it is Circus Grimm's wicked logic; nobody is going to miss or search for a homeless pauper, and thieves will get thrown in prison anyway so why not just throw them into their 'prisons' instead and get some more freaks in the process? When Circus Grimm catches you in the act of stealing from them or stowing away in one of their carriages, they throw you into the werewolves' cage and let the hungry beasts do the rest. It's a painful death, but if you're still alive after they're done with you then you become one of us…and like I said before, once you're in the troupe, you die in it.

The dog-fights are always vicious and bloody. This is what they want to see; they bet money on our lives like betting on racehorses, they force us to fight to the death so that they can win scraps of paper and small pieces of metal...what is a brutal bloodbath for us is just a fun game for them. I don't understand; if it's so much fun then why don't they jump into the ring and join in the 'fun'? Why do we have to 'have fun' for them? What is so entertaining about watching us massacre each other? I hate this game. I have murdered many of my own kin; I never lose at this blood sport and I hate that fact, yet I still keep winning. I don't have any choice; if I refuse to fight they whip me and if I let my opponent win they will kill me. Then again, death would be a reward for me...but the unforgiving grip of the moon forbids it. Its cursed light feeds our desperation to survive, whether we want to or not, as if the moon itself is a spectator gambling with our lives. And it seems to always deem me as the favourite to win. Here I'm not doomed to die...I am doomed to live.

For years I have been the reigning champion of the fighting ring. I've never lost a fight, even when the Ringmaster's tried to rig them. I'm not sure how I've survived for as long as I have done; I don't know if it's something to do with different breeds of lycanthrope being better than others or just sheer luck, but it's really difficult trying to think about that when you have a goliath of an animal rabidly clawing at your face. Yes, they always aim for your face – they'll do their best to gouge your eyes out or break your jaw. You can't fight if you can't see or bite. That's why I aim for their face as well. I don't show mercy because they don't show me any. I don't even pray for them anymore; it's pointless to, because what kind of God would allow any of this to happen? But I do kill them quickly. I don't leave my defeated opponent to die slowly and painfully. I always end my fights by breaking their necks with either my teeth or hands; it's the very least I can do to end their suffering.

Tonight is no exception, especially since my latest victim is so young and inexperienced…this is this pup's first dog-fight. I can tell that he's never fought an older and more dominant wolf before. He comes at me full of determination but his overconfidence outweighs his common sense. While he puts up a good fight, he lacks skill, thus I end up making a dog's dinner of him, just like many others before him.

I clamp my mouth around his nearly maneless neck and thrash my head side to side violently, then finish him off by crushing his windpipe between my jaws. It makes a horrible squelchy crunching noise when I do and I taste the hot tang of blood on my tongue as I break skin. I tear away the poor pup's throat, his blood and flesh hanging from between my teeth. Blood spurts from the large hole made in his neck as he jerks and flails for a little bit before finally dying.

The audience clap wildly as if they are cheering for a victorious Roman Gladiator. Another full moon and another execution over and done with until next month. The keepers quickly remove the loser's corpse from the ring while the Clowns keep the crowd distracted – they don't want them to see the dead pup's body transform back into the human boy he once was…The audience finally leaves, some disappointed and penniless, while others will be doing cartwheels tonight, thanks to the new riches my painful victory has won for them. Once again I receive no gratitude from anyone for my services, only a sore aching body and yet more scars to add to its collection. But as the moon wanes so does my rage. As soon as the show is finished I collapse from exhaustion.

I wake up only to find myself back in my jail, all shackled up for the remainder of the night, curtains pulled all around my cage to hide me from the morning's light. My wounds have been bandaged tightly while I was unconscious and a plate has been placed beside me filled to the brim with huge juicy chunks of red, raw meat. My prize for surviving yet another dog-fight. I am so hungry but I am too tired and weak to even lift my head up to sniff it. All I want to do is rest. I shuffle a bit, trying to find a position where I'm not putting any weight on one of my injuries, then once I'm comfortable I close my eyes and drift off to sleep.

But tonight, something stirs me from my slumber, a rather suspicious conversation that catches my attention. I pretend to be asleep but I listen carefully. The lazy keepers have left an open crack between the curtains so I can take a sly peak outside, and I hear everything clearly word for word. It is the Ringmaster and the Landlord arguing. I don't know the full details since I only overheard a little of the story from the clowns, but somehow the Ringmaster was able to con this drunkard farmer into providing the circus lodging for the whole winter. However, from what I hear it appears that the foolish Ringmaster had promised the Landlord payment for the rent but has paid nothing for three months. Moron. The Landlord already loathes this circus just as much as I do, and now he has lost his patience with its leader, he is demanding the rent to be paid this week...so the Ringmaster is making a new offer, a wager, and a dangerous one at that.

The lunar eclipse is this week. He will arrange another fight just for the occasion, and if the lead animal wins then all the money placed on the loser will pay for the rent. By lead animal...he means me! Is the bloody fool insane?! The Lunar eclipse is only two nights away and I am still injured from tonight's show. There is no way my injuries will heal in time! The damn idiot has gone too far but it is too late to protest; the deal has been struck as the two pigs in gentlemen's clothing shake hands on it. Besides...it's not as if either of them would heed my plea for them to see common sense anyway...after all, when did a pig ever listen? Especially to a wolf.

For the next two days I do my best to speed up my recovery; I remain as still as possible to reserve energy, I finish all my meals even when not hungry to build up strength, and I drink heavily from my water bowl and from the rain which I secretly collect in a rusty pail next to my cage, to keep me hydrated and wash out my insides. Of course my efforts are simply not enough; one can only do so much to heal themselves without proper medical care. The Ringmaster's also trying to make me heal faster by dropping me from the show for a while, however, he's not trying too hard since the greedy money-hoarder won't spend a single penny on medicine for a mere animal that he can replace whenever he wants. On the other hand…what doctor is brave or brainless enough to even attempt to treat the wounds of a werewolf?

Time soon runs out for me: the lunar eclipse doesn't wait for me to recover. Tonight's the night and just as I predicted, I stand no chance. The keepers practically shove me into the ring tonight; I fill with anxiety when I lock eyes with my latest challenger. My opponent is a new addition to the freak show, bought on short notice from an auction on the black market. He is large and healthy and, above all, strong. There was never any doubt who was going to win this fight, but the audience don't care – they have paid for a show and a show is what they are going to get. We get the match started the usual way we do: a few roars at each other and the customary howl, trying to intimidate each other with the strength of our voices. I am much louder than the new werewolf, but it doesn't mean anything right now. Just a bluff and we both know it. Then we charge at each other; now the fight has truly begun.

I bound towards the other wolf and leap for the tree-trunk thickness of his throat as he does the same. We collide with each other in mid jump and land with a heavy thud, and then roll around the floor in a flurry of fur, claws and fangs, biting and scratching one another. We break free from each other's deadly embrace only to ram into each other again, slamming our whole bodies together repeatedly. I twist clear when he lunges for me for the fifth time and retreat backwards until my back almost touches the cage's bars. I'm battered and bruised all over; blood is spilling from every claw mark and bite mark in my flesh.

I know it's pointless but still I try my best to survive and maintain my title – again my instincts drive me onward to compete for dominance. It is no use...my body is too broken from the last show; each time I move, pain shoots through every limb like lightning, pain that amplifies whenever my opponent strikes me. My claws swing at him and they miss, his claws swing at me and they hit. I bite him hard, he bites me harder. I try to move fast but he moves faster. If I was at full strength there would've been hope for a tie, but as I am now there is no hope.

The fight ends quickly; a sound blow to my skull knocks me to ground, my lungs heave for air and my muscles tremble as blood pours down my face from an ugly gash made across my brow. My eyes roll from the impact of the smack and I am rendered so dizzy that I feel like my skull has just been cracked. But somehow, despite my wooziness, I still manage to look up above me and see my conqueror just as he smashes into my flank, pressing me down. I try to roll free but I'm pinned down hard against the floor. With one foot still pressing down on my neck he stands over me and raises his bloodied paw up in the air, readying to swing it down and smear my guts all over the sawdust ring. I don't bother getting back up. I want this to be over with. It is not just the fight and my title as champion I have lost, but also my will to live. Please let my death be quick.

But death is not granted to me. A deafening bang brings silence to the Ring. A single stray bullet to the head swiftly ends the life of my would-be executioner, and his limp corpse falls on top of me. The crowd start to boo and hiss while the circus' staff tries to gain control of the situation. I hear only garbled shouting blurred by the perpetuous ringing in my ears caused by the gunshot, so I can't understand a single word anyone is yelling.

The keepers take advantage of my weakened and dazed state to drag me out of the ring and back to my cage without any need for restraints or drugs. I show no resistance whatsoever as my mind is too overwhelmed with confusion. Who shot at us? I thought 'circus animals' were dispensable and easily replaced, so why am I being saved? Or rather...am I truly being saved, or just being robbed once again of my only way out of this cruel limbo? It could still be my bestial instincts thinking for me right now, because I'm not sure if I should show thanks to the mystery gunman or rip their throat out if I ever meet them...

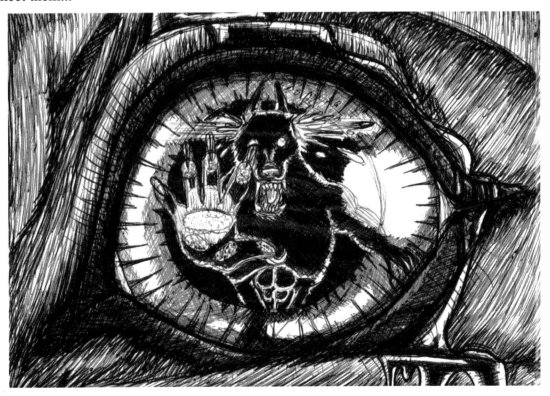

ACT IIII

The eclipse has now passed and the moon's light is free to taunt me again. I don't care much about it right now. I pace up and down restlessly in my cage like a deranged lion. The eclipse is over but the effects of the full moon two nights ago are still gripping my senses. Under normal circumstances I should feel relieved that I am alive, but instead I just feel outrage, angry that I didn't win the fight on fair terms. Angry that I was not allowed to die and my victor was not allowed to live. If he was to die it was supposed to be by my hands: that is the law of nature, and that law was broken. I am so pent up with mixed emotions and energy that I have lost the pain in my limbs that crippled me in the ring tonight.

It takes a sudden bash against my bars to snap me out of my deep thought. It's the Landlord, drunk again. He is brushing his bottle of whiskey across the bars as he stares at me. He spits at me and I slash at him through the bars for it. He stumbles back and spills his whiskey all down his shirt. He curses then slumps down on a hay-bail to drink deeper into his own misery. Must be blaming me for the spoilt fight. Because of the refunds, he didn't get nearly enough money for his rent.

Just now another familiar figure comes along; it is Corny, the lead clown. He joins the Landlord for a drink...but something's off. Something that disturbs me. I smell fresh gunpowder on him. I also smell liquor on his breath, and sense great frustration in his voice as he rants on about his own misfortune to his new ally. Apparently it is not just me the Ringmaster is seemingly trying to replace; Corny was informed this morning that he has been dropped as the main act to make way for a new attraction involving steam-powered machinery. The farmer may be oblivious, but to me this sounds like the perfect motive for Corny, my most common tormentor, to want to sabotage my act to humiliate the Ringmaster...and me.

My anger builds as the scent of smoke from a gun confirms the identity of my saboteur, but I feel an alarming sense of unease as the two men drink on. The three of us here are all united in our hate for the circus but Corny's lips are getting looser and the conversation is getting more irate. An animal knows more about the world than what we let on; I know that something bad is going to happen. Though I don't know what, again instincts are powerful things. Suddenly a small shining light literally catches my eye. I look to a barrel beside my cage and see a set of keys; Corny must've just left them there before he joined the Landlord. Could one of those keys...possibly be one that opens my prison? It seems almost too good to be true; I have tried countless times to escape in the past, but either failed or had only a very short-lived freedom before quickly being hunted down and caught again. My attempts were foiled so many times that I gave up and accepted my life as it is.

However, this time the keys are right in front of me and their keeper is too drunk and too busy complaining to notice...I cautiously reach for them and my claws hook them quietly. They may not even be the right keys to my cage, but I cannot let such a hopeful chance slip by when my prey are distracted by their bitter whiskey and their even more bitter hatred...

A few sips more and Corny seals all our fates, including his own, by letting slip the ultimate fumble of words; 'the Ringmaster is a cheat, an illusionist and a master of cards'.

Now knowing that he had been cheated out of his money and tricked into giving lodgings for the circus, the landlord works himself into a rage, frightening even the drunken clown. I am now frantically attacking my locks with the keys. I can see the bloodthirst in his eyes and sense his heartbeat racing; I know there is going to be bloodshed soon, so it is now or never. I free myself from my chains and unlock my cage's door just in time to see the Landlord reaching for his pitchfork. Corny panics and tries to stop him, but his pleas fall on deaf ears. The farmer wants revenge, and so do I.

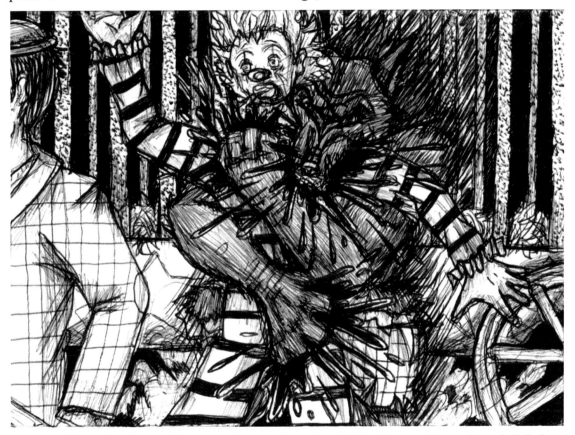

In a blind fury he shoves Corny against my bars, but before he can thrust that pitchfork into him I steal his opportunity. With an almighty push I swing open the door and pounce upon the startled clown. I dig my claws in and sink my teeth deep into his flesh, swallowing his hot blood gushing into my mouth, the taste sending me into a feeding frenzy. I am exultant; his flailing limbs bring me into a wild state of euphoria. Yes! Oh yes! Oh how I've missed the taste of the delicious pain of another! I have missed the excitement of a real kill! It has been so long since I last devoured a wicked pig's flesh, and best of all: I am eating one of the pigs who has caused me the most suffering. *Ha ha ha, this is for all the whipping! This is for all the jokes and sneers! Not laughing now, are you? No, you're screaming now, and it is music to my ears! Scream! Scream for me, clown! More! I want to hear your music more! Scream as I eat you alive!*

As I feast, I peer ahead to meet the eyes of the surprised Landlord. He stares at me emotionless. I glare back at him with a guttural snarl, daring him to try and take my prey from me...but he simply smirks, ignoring Corny's dying cries for help, and with his pitchfork in hand he turns his back on us to set out for his own score to settle. As I watch him casually walk away, all I can think to myself is that he would make a good werewolf...

I leave the messy pulp of what is left of Corny in the barn. He and I are the first two dominoes to fall in the series of murderous events to follow. Thanks to all the times I have spent in chains, I have learned to be stealthy as I used to have to avoid making the metal rings jingle and rattle. I sneak in the shadows silently and swiftly, and even when spotted I quickly dispose of whoever sees me before they can reach for any means of a weapon or raise the alarm. First rule of killing is to never let the prey scream. Not even the Alsatian and Rottweiler guard-dogs are a match for me when I'm unchained and empowered by meat and moonlight. This is it. I am escaping tonight, and this time nothing is going to stop me. It's convenient for me that the circus was set up on farmland; farms mean fields, fields mean crops, and crops mean shelter in the darkness. I spot the perfect escape route: a complicated maze of tall corn plants. If I slip through the corn without breaking any of the stalks and without making too much noise, I can reach the woods beyond the fields way before anyone notices my empty cage. And by the time they've searched the whole farm and all the fields, I will already be long gone.

I slow down and carefully manoeuvre my way around the untidy piles of farming tools and towers of crates full of the circus' equipment. I crawl beneath the other cages as quietly as I can so as not to wake up the animals and other werewolves. If they do awaken then they will start crying out and trying to break free themselves, and doing that would most definitely draw attention to where I am and my final attempt of escape will fail. I simply cannot allow that.

A couple of the other wolves and a lion stir a little when they catch the tiniest whiff of my scent, but since they can't see where I am they pay it no mind and go back to sleep. I feel sorry for them; I wish I could set the others free as well, and the riot they'd start would probably make a good distraction too…but I left the keys back in my cage and I don't have time to just rush back for them.

I stop just beneath the cage of the elephants and scan the surroundings. My eyes are naturally designed for nocturnal activity which makes it easy for me to observe the area without a light. The entrance into the cornfields is just a yard away from me, but before I have a chance to make a dash for it I spot a man's shadow coming my way.

Quickly I hide behind a haystack. I peer around the side to see the loathsome Ringmaster; he is looking around with a lamp, calling for Corny. Damn it, I was hoping he wouldn't have noticed the lead clown's absence so soon. However, while I'm debating in my head whether to just wait until he goes away or maul him like I have already done with Corny and a few other obstacles tonight, I hear heavy footsteps fast approaching. In his pursuit across the farm, the Landlord has finally found the cheating scoundrel he'd been searching for.

I remain hidden behind the large haystack as he encounters his target. Despite his protests and appeals to the angered farmer thirsty for blood, the Ringmaster meets his maker...The Landlord's sharp pitchfork pierces the Ringmaster's neck like a pencil through tissue, and he collapses into a bloody heap on a hay-bale.

The strong scent of my enslaver's blood is dizzying. I actually find it a bit unfair...I wanted to kill him too. He's done far worse things to me than merely cheating at a card game; why do you have more right than me to kill him? But as I watch the satisfied farmer smugly stroll away with the Ringmaster's lamp and a peculiar grin on his face, I see the Ringmaster's chest still rising and falling weakly. The prey is still alive? Incompetent drunken amateur, can't even commit murder properly he's that drunk! Or perhaps...he has left him like this on purpose? Well played, my sadistic friend. I step out from my hiding spot and salivate at the sight of the pitchforked man. I lick my lips clean of the blood smeared all around my mouth; my belly still has room for dessert and it's never good to leave a meal or a job unfinished...

I slowly approach him. He hears my footsteps and weakly turns his head towards the owner of them. He doesn't seem panicked by my presence, but his eyes look glazed and disorientated, so I guess his vision must be blurry from blood loss. Of course in the darkness of night and without the light of his taken lamp, it's even harder to see me. I move closer and loom over him. He reaches his arms out to me. With the pitchfork embedded deep into his neck and chest, I can imagine how difficult it must be to so much as breathe; but still he tries speaking to me. He's begging me to save him. I can't help but utter the tiniest chuckle now. Poor fool doesn't know who I am, he thinks I'm here to help him. HA! Boy he couldn't be more wrong. I answer his pleas with a growl but the growl does not come from my throat; I am so hungry for his blood that my stomach is growling impatiently, demanding to be filled. I shall obey it.

The Ringmaster's pale face turns paler as he realises too late who it is towering over him. The small hope in his eyes quickly turns to terror as he now feebly struggles with the pitchfork, trying to pry it out of his body. But it has him pinned down to the hay-bale, and the fork is too slippery with his own blood for him to grip it properly.

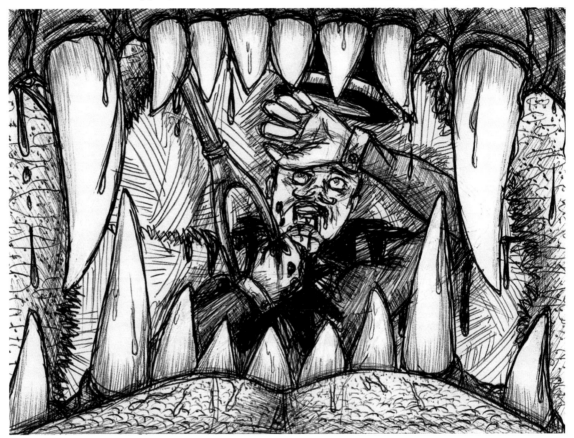

He can't get away from me so instead he tries pleading to me. As if I'm going to spare him; he is wasting his last breath. He has put me through unspeakable tortures, forced me to do horrible things that will haunt me for the rest of my life. The blood he has spilled and made me spill all these years can never be undone. Why should I spare him? He doesn't deserve to be spared. After all this villainous conman has done unto me, how can he possibly expect me to show him any tiny shred of sympathy?

I fall on him. I ravage him ravenously. He squeals like a frightened little piglet one last time and I simply ignore it; just like he used to ignore all of my cries of pain. I ignore his wet hands pushing, punching and scratching my face. I ignore his spindly legs kicking my stomach and groin, I ignore it all with a cold sneer on my face. It is too late to apologise to me and it is far too late to atone for your sins; there is no bargain you can make that will save your skin...All you can do now, pitiful Sir, is repent and pray that the devil shows you more mercy than me.

ACT IV

My torturer is dead: I have eaten him and the circus is now leaderless. There is definitely no going back now; the rest of the circus will kill me for this (then again, they'll probably secretly hail me a hero for ridding them of such a greedy slave-driver for a boss). Don't get me wrong though, I actually hate the taste and would rather eat rotten carrion, but I have no choice...animals don't eat for pleasure, only for survival. It is an instinct long forgotten by man but still reigning strong in the rest of God's and Satan's creations. That same instinct rules over my kind too. I have been starved all week; I need all the energy I can get if I want to escape, so right now it's either me or them. Any port in a storm as they say (and I would be lying if I said that I didn't enjoy butchering my imprisoner). Besides, if I don't eat my prey then I risk passing on my curse to them even in death, and I would rather not grant my enemies power and immortality...it's bad enough that I'm a monster already, and myself is enough – I don't need any more monsters in my life.

Now with both the Farmer and Ringmaster finally gone, I leap into the cornfield. I make sure not to land in any mud or break any stalks; I can't leave any footprints or other evidence that would lead hunters to me. I avoid the clear paths that are accessible as it would defeat the point of hiding if I used the open trails; I would be spotted quickly and it'd be easier for my captors to chase me on clear open ground. The stalks will get in the way of them. Problem is, they get in my way too. I am resisting the strong urge to just rip them away with my claws; I must stick to the plan, leave no tracks and make no noise. It is tempting to drop down and run off on all fours, but if I want to outsmart hunters and their dogs then I need to keep whatever little tracks I do leave as faint and confusing as possible. But being caught by hunters suddenly becomes the least of my worries as I smell smoke forming above me. The air grows warmer and not in a natural way, as it is the wrong season for warm nights. A sense of new danger arises in me at the sounds of panicking people.

I take a brief glance behind me and see fire, lots of fire, burning everything it touches. So this is why the Landlord stole the Ringmaster's lamp; this is without a doubt that drunken madman's doing. To try and erase all the evidence of his crime, as well as further punish the circus for conning him out of his money and his dignity, he's thrown that lamp at something flammable, smashed it upon impact and the lamp's spilled oil has helped whatever the lamp hit catch fire.

The air is suffocating me with heat and smoke. The hot air stings my eyes and the smoke blinds me in this maze, and if that's not problematic enough, the scorching air also burns my nostrils and all I can smell now is smoke and fried corn. I can feel some of the flames singe the ends of the fur on my tail and thighs; the fire's quickly catching up to me. This is far worse than the time the Ringmaster made me jump through five burning hoops all in one leap. FIVE! I was covered in bald patches from where the hoops had burnt me for three months after I did that. If I let this blazing fire engulf me, it will be more than just my fur that will get incinerated.

I've never run this fast in all my life. I'm panting and gasping for breath so hard that my chest is stinging. My aching feet are so sore from sprinting across uneven rocky earth without rest. I feel like my legs are about to give in at any moment, but I keep running regardless. I did not make it this far just to get lost and killed in a burning maze; as God is my witness, I'll either die a free beast...or fry trying.

I keep on running without stopping or looking back. I dare not. At least, not until I'm free. The heat is unbearable; I feel as if I'm inside an oven. Now I know what a hotdog must feel like. I am so hot that I'm truly scared that I might just faint right now. Again survival instincts are incredibly powerful. Before, I used to curse them whenever I wanted to kill myself out of desperation for freedom of any kind, but this time my survival instincts are working for me, not against me. They are driving forward and keeping me alive for as long as possible. I must keep running; I have to get out of here, or else all my efforts will be in vain.

Despite the burning air and smothering smoke hindering my sight and sense of smell, I somehow make it out of the maze at last, just before the flames can consume me along with the corn plants. I am amazed that I don't have a single burn on me, but I am not out of danger just yet and I waste no time in using my reserved strength to throw myself onward in a sudden acceleration of speed. I am running so fast that I think I'm outrunning the Grim Reaper himself.

I see the way out of the fields dead ahead of me, the exit out of the farmlands. It is blocked by a tall gate but that does not faze me. Once I am close enough I hurdle over it almost effortlessly. I'm far away enough now I think, so I risk taking a look over my shoulder. I see the farm and the Circus in the far distance behind me, both burning to the ground.

The screams of the people and animals burning with the Circus slowly die down until there is only the sound of crackling flames and collapsing foundations. I appear to be the only survivor...I cannot help but feel a pang of guilt about that. I abandoned the other freaks to save myself, including my own kin. Did I have the right to do that? Then again, would they have helped me or done the same as me if given my current situation? Too late to do anything about it now; the circus is already almost fully cremated. At least my fellow tormented freaks are free from that hell, and our enslavers burned alive in their own hell that they created for us. A fitting end if you ask me.

Even after entering the woods, I don't stop running and I don't look back a second time. Better safe than sorry; can't risk anything if there are any survivors of the fire other than me. I must've been running for hours because the sky is starting to turn a light shade of blue and the sparrows have started singing. I run and run until I cannot run anymore, then I walk and walk until I cannot walk anymore, so I drop down onto all fours and crawl...until I can't even crawl anymore. I have reached a limit not possible for any human or animal. My limbs refuse to move another inch; they buckle and cave in beneath me, and I collapse on the grass with a soft thud in a safe cluster of shrubs and bushes. My whole body at this point has turned numb from both the cold air and constant aching in my tired muscles. My heavy eyelids slowly seal shut as my resistance vanishes and I finally succumb to sleep, but the last thing I see before I close my eyes is the moon, shining through the roof of leaves and branches above me as if it's trying to find me but can't, because of the trees and bushes. The moon would be beautiful tonight if it wasn't for tonight's terrible events.

That same night I have a dream. I dream of what was and of what might be. It's the first time in a very long time that I am not seeing the ghosts of my victims. In my dream now, I am in an endless maze of corn. The further I run inside it the taller the corn seems to grow. Above me is not the sky but instead fire, and chasing after me are the clowns and keepers led by the Ringmaster, but they are hideously disfigured.

The clowns' faces are melting like candle wax, exposing bone. The keepers' skins are horribly charred like burnt bacon, and the Ringmaster is almost unrecognisable…just a blob of bloody half-digested meat with a wicked face and a top hat. They are laughing hysterically at me like hungry hyenas, calling my efforts futile and saying I belong to them, that I should burn with them. I refuse to listen and just keep running.

I see the exit in front of me at last, a giant version of the farm's gate I leaped over before, and on the other side of it I see a bright light. Just like before, I use all the strength left in my body and jump over the big gate. The light swallows me and everything falls unnaturally silent…but there is no ground beneath me and I then start to plummet into darkness again, falling and falling but there is no bottom. The light above me, however, seems to be fixed on me like a show's spotlight…but the show is over.

Dawn approaches and the rising sun's light shines through the green bushes, sheltering me. Though I do not waken (not fully anyway), I still feel the light warming my skin ticklishly. It is comforting and refreshing at first, until it brings upon me an alien sensation I have not felt for a long time.

My limbs cramp up and my body shivers as it begins to shrink. My fur sheds from my skin and falls to the ground in large clumps of matted coarse hair. My now hairless tail pulls itself back into my spine. My fangs drop out one by one as smaller teeth push them out of my bleeding gums, and my jaws pull back into my flattening face and lock in place. My claws uncurl and straighten as they retract back into my slimming fingers.

Shredded remains of clothing still tangled around me that felt tight before now feel very loose and baggy on me. It feels as though I am being choked, smothered, like my power is being drained from my flesh, leaving me weak and helpless. The night is over. It is morning now, and I am human again.

Cold and half naked on the damp grass, I remain there for a while, trying to will my heartbeat to slow down. The reversion process is more painful and requires more stamina than the actual transformation into the monster...both physically and mentally. Spots of colour start to speckle my vision now that the changing of forms is complete.

I blink as I try to clear my vision. I hold up my hands to stare at the pink, hairless skin, and flex my scarred wrists. I am surprised that I have no other scars, despite how many times I have fought other wolves in the circus ring. Then again, a lycanthrope's metabolism is much faster than a normal human's or animal's. I guess that's one good thing about this curse.

The light that was denied to me for years feels so wonderful on my body. I am still in total disbelief of all of this; for years I have dreamed of being free…I had tried so many times to escape and always failed each time…but not this time. I don't know how or why fate decided now was the best time to succeed, but I couldn't care less. Better late than never. If I could remember how to…I would smile.

My throat is hoarse and my mouth is so dry. Having such a high metabolism also means you feel hungry and thirsty so much quicker than the norm, even after already having a large meal just moments ago. The first thing to do that is on my mind is find something to drink, to rehydrate myself and replenish lost energy.

Once I feel ready I force myself up from the ground and stagger onto my feet. I am very unsteady standing up. I feel like a baby taking its first steps, as though this is my first time walking on two legs. Being back in human form after years of being inside the body of a wolf, and crammed into a cage that was much too small for a beast of my size at the time, is going to take quite some time getting used to again. I stumble and hobble out from the bushes and go in search of any source of water. I trip a couple of times, but my sensitive nose and sharp hearing soon lead me to the smell of water-lilies and the sound of fish-filled water. A lake.

The water is remarkably clear but I am so thirsty that I don't give a damn whether it is fresh or not. I drop down on my knees and waste no time in bringing my face to the lake's water and sucking in as much as I can swallow through my cracked lips. The icy water hits my stomach like a kick in the guts, but my thirst is too strong for me to care. I get some algae stuck on my cheeks and wipe it off but accidentally smear mud across my face as I do. I was in such awe of being human once more that I forgot that I was still caked in mud with bits of corn stuck in my hair. I also notice that my fingers and palms of my hands are painted red with dried blood: reminders of what I had done to sate my hunger for justice and vengeance, of what lengths I had gone to so I could escape that hell called Circus Grimm. This time I can't decide whether I should feel proud or guilty for my ghastly deeds.

I close my eyes as I cup my hands in the water to collect some to wash myself with. A strangled gasp leaves my mouth as I splash the liquid into my face and over my head. It is like ice. Purifying ice. I swallow in a big mouthful of air and hold my breath as I then dunk my whole head into the lake.

I swish it about for a quick moment underwater before yanking myself from the liquid with a gasp for breath and throwing my head back, whipping my wet hair back and forth to free it from the algae, as well as any remaining dirt from the corn maze. I want and need to feel clean...but the harsh truth is that once your hands are stained with the blood of another, they will never be clean ever again. However, the feeling of water soaking my skin and drying with the windy breeze is so relaxing. It feels chilly but the light from the unclouded sun keeps me warm enough to stop me shivering.

I am enjoying this feeling…I am feeling more alive now than I ever did before in my life. After washing my skin tenderly I take a look at myself in the shining surface of the lake. My dazed eyes widen in shock.

The circus always kept me in the dark to trick my body into believing that it was always night time, to keep me trapped in a wolf's body so that people would only see me as an animal and not as a person. But now it's daylight and I'm not a wolf. I have not seen my own reflection for so long that I hardly recognise myself. With a soft bewildered whimper I feel my face with trembling fingers and examine my mirror image. How old am I? Was my skin always so pale? Has my hair always been this long? When did I get so big? How long exactly have I been wearing these same ripped, bloodstained trousers for? Just...who am I? When your own reflection is a stranger to you, you know for damn well sure that you've been in hell for a long, LONG time.

I wander for days in these vast woods. Not because I am lost, but because I have nowhere else to go. I can't go back to the circus; not that I would ever want to in a hundred centuries, even if I was paid to...but I can't go home either, because I have no clue where home is. How can I go home if I can't remember it? For now I am living in a haze, not knowing what else to do but to focus on survival. There is nothing I can do until I overcome my amnesia. The circus has wrecked and ruined my mind though. Even now I am still its prisoner, reliving it all in my dreams every night. No full moon, however, so I can get some means of rest at least. I keep telling myself that it's all just a dream now, but it doesn't change anything. The circus happened. It was real.

The days turn into weeks, and I am still no closer to figuring out who I was before the circus broke me. I have recovered some bits and pieces of memory, but they are only trivial things like how to read, how to write, how to talk...but nothing really important. I still can't even remember my own name. I have travelled great distances now; even risked walking through countryside and cutting across fields to reach another forest. I pass a few hikers and sometimes little children. They try talking to me but I ignore them. Behind me I hear them whispering amongst themselves in fear, saying that I must be a ghost or a witch.

Whenever I see hunters, I hide. In my experience, hunters know a wolf when they see one – they'd shoot me on sight. I often pass groups of woodcutters working away in the forest but I stay clear of them, because I know exactly what they'll think of me if they see me. A woman wearing nothing but ripped, dirty pants must be a gypsy or a prostitute, or perhaps an escaped slave. To society those three things are disgusting and to be avoided...but to lonely men with frigid old wives, working to the bones day in day out for pitiful money that can't even buy bread; such a young vulnerable girl all alone in the woods who nobody will miss...is a rare, delicious meal on a gold plate.

One of them spotted me once and actually grabbed a rope then started to follow me, but thankfully when I ran he didn't bother to continue his 'hunt'. Revolting perverted pigs. One day, however, while walking along a cobblestone road hidden by overgrown grass, I come across an abandoned camp. Looks like whoever was here before me left in a hurry: the tents are still here and there's leftover food, still warm in a pot over the dying campfire. Gypsies or Bandits maybe? It doesn't seem like anyone is coming back, so this is a good opportunity to eat something I don't have to chase and kill for once. I shan't stay though; I can't say for sure this campsite is entirely abandoned. If somebody does come back I'll be in trouble. But I won't waste a chance to cover my nudity now. I shred the cloth from one of the tents to fashion myself a blanket to cloak myself with and then hurry away...But as I do; something flashes in my mind.

A very powerful image provided by the familiarity of this cloth's warmth and texture. I'm remembering something. Something important. I wore a cloak once...as a child...a white cloak with a hood. It was a present...given to me by someone taller than me...but I can't see their face. Some more memories return. I see two little girls – one is wearing my cloak and the other...I don't know what the other child looks like properly; she's very blurry in my mind, just like the person who gave me that cloak...I also see a house, a cottage I think. It stands out the most in my fragmented memories, as if it's bathed in light. Is it my cottage? Is that where I used to live? I try my hardest to remember but I just end up giving myself a sharp headache. Oh well, I guess my memories will return eventually. I just have to give them time. But that house...and my white cloak...I know they're important, but why?

I don't realise that I've still been walking this entire time whilst trying to remember, until I nearly walk right into a sign post. I look up and try to read it but the text is all worn out and scratched off. The wood is rotten and covered in cobwebs, so this signpost is pretty old. I can't avoid people forever; if I ever want to have a real life then I will need to return to civilisation at some point, and maybe wherever this sign is pointing to is someplace I can find more keys to unlocking the memories I actually want back.

ACT V

Needless to say that this is a very old road I am now following. Must've been walking for hours by now and still not a single sign of people in sight, other than the cobblestones I'm walking on. I have left the forest while following this forgotten path; it is just a green blur in the far distance behind me now. But still no sign of civilisation to be found: not so much as a field to indicate any farms, not even another signpost since the very one that pointed me this way in the first place. I look to the sky; the sun is starting to set. Tonight is the right night for my 'cycle'...I'd better keep moving, try to cover as much ground as possible before nightfall.

Eventually I reach a rather big moor. I see fences but there are no animals behind them and the wood is mouldy with the paint all peeled off. There are no people now but at least this is evidence to prove there were some in the past. So I know that I am going in the right direction. Should reach a village or town soon, if people used to live here; people rarely travel too far from their origins. And speaking of origins...as I reach a hill I feel that same sudden stabbing sensation in my head that I felt miles back at the abandoned campsite, but this time it is so strong that I wince and clutch my head.

I blink just once but when I open my eyes I do not see the moor I know now, I see the moor anew...sheep and cows grazing all around me, and those two girls, again giggling and running up the clean cobblestones hand in hand. I see them both much clearer than before; they are twins. I remember another important memory...I had a twin sister...I wore a little cloak and she always wore a silver crucifix. We wore them because people used to say it was the only real way to tell us two apart. But wait...a crucifix? That's not right. It was my sister's. So why is it around my neck right now? I am not mistaken: this definitely belongs to my sister; that I can remember clearly. Come to think of it...where is my white cloak? I never saw it anywhere at the circus...where is my cloak and why am I wearing my sister's crucifix?

My train of thought comes flying off the tracks as my flashback is shattered by a hideous odour and a just as repulsing voice to match. Someone is calling to me and not in a pleasant manner at all. Scared that it might possibly be someone from the circus again, I hastily turn to face the figure, but I relax a little to see it isn't so. But I am still concerned by his perverted grin and failing attempt at forming seductive sentences. A tramp or poacher probably; he is dirty like one. I ignore him and turn to leave. Suddenly his words of lust turn into words of anger. I hear him growl: *"don't ya dare turn yer back on me! I'm gonna enjoy tasting you!"*

I quicken my pace and he quickens his. He is definitely stalking me. I start running but not because of him...because the moon is rising. I can feel my heart race and my muscles twitch. My body begins to burn up and my mouth starts hurting as I feel my jaws readying to accommodate the rows of fangs yet to grow.

However, I don't think running is necessary anymore, as my stalker's voice changes from sleazy to demonic and his stench changes to a scent I know all too well. I look over my shoulder and see his shape twisting and growing, and hair sprouting from every inch of his skin. His stained cotton shirt stretches and stretches until the seams pull apart as his hairy chest expands. His ribcage deepens then pushes itself out like a Greyhound's. He rips off most of his tatty clothes the best he can with his fattening hands. His fingernails lengthen, twist and harden into curved spikes. He falls onto all fours, then almost giddily raises himself back up onto his hind legs and stares at me hungrily as he licks his drooling chops. Are you bloody kidding me? Of all the things to run into at this time of the month, it's another werewolf? What kind of sick joke is this? So when he said he wanted to taste me, he meant it literally. Now under normal circumstances a young maiden should scream and run. But I'm not normal, am I? He thinks he's dealing with some mere mortal girl, does he? Well he can think again, because I am a predator too and I am tired of running!

The moonlight bathes my sweaty skin like icy water. My shaky breathing gets more ragged and a tiny electric spark ignites inside me. It tickles and warms me, like an internal itch and there's no way of scratching it. It's maddening. The burning heat pumping through my body is so hot that it feels as though my bones are melting. My heart is pounding so hard against my ribcage that it hurts. The pain is delicious; it's so irresistible that I could just cry out with pain and frustration right about now. I hyperventilate as the full moon's gaze sends spasms of sheer exhilaration shooting through every fibre of my being. Time's up; the change has begun.

As soon as I too begin to return to my own bestial form, the vagabond freezes, suddenly uncertain and confused. My skull thickens and my face broadens. My dark hazel eyes turn into a petrifying greenish gold and glow demonically. I groan uncontrollably as my limbs begin to stretch and bulge, and I whine in agony as my muscles tear and ripple. Thin streams of blood run down my blackening lips as large ivory fangs rip through my gums, forcing all of my human teeth out of my mouth as my jaws stretch into a wolfish snout. Each tooth falls to the cobblestone ground like little blood-coated marbles. They are tiny compared to my new razor-sharp, tusk-like canines. I dig my claws into my paw-padded palms; my once delicate slender hands are now massive club-like paws. A long, bony tail grows from the bottom of my spine and fattens with a mass of bushy fur. It hurts, all this changing of my body; it hurts so much. Not just physically either; my brain is being devoured by the beast inside me. I can't hold it in anymore. I scream…but my scream breaks apart. It drops like an elevator through registers of distorted sounds and becomes a deafening howl.

I fall to my knees, fatigued from the stress my body has undergone to metamorphose into the creature whose shape I now take. Both of us are now fully transformed. My back is still turned on him but I hear him sniffing and grunting. Obviously his intentions before were to eat me...but now he is clueless about what to do. I don't think he's ever seen another werewolf before.

He suddenly bites my tail. Only once. He's trying to assert dominance. I barely feel his teeth; it is more like a nip than anything else. He growls but when I growl louder he immediately falls quiet. I've just had enough...I'm sick of running and fighting, fighting and running; it's all I've ever done for as long as I can remember. I finally stand up and turn to face him...and my entire being fills to the brim with ungodly anger the very instant my gaze meets his. I know him...It's *him*. It's *HIM!*

I roar at him with all the air in my lungs and I swear the ground trembles with the force of my voice. He whimpers and tucks his thin tail between his equally thin legs. My bellowing roar knocks him to the ground as easy as blowing down a house made of straw, and he tries to crawl away from me...but I won't let him get away with his crimes anymore. I grab him by the tail and drag him back towards me; he yelps or rather screams at me like a terrified little piglet, as he tries to claw at my hands...just like I did when he grabbed me many years ago. His shrieks and pitiful yowls remind me of when I was once begging him to let me go. He doesn't remember me, but I remember him! I remember now! I remember everything! *It's all your fault! You did this to me! How could you?! I was just a little girl! I'd done nothing wrong! Why?! WHY?! TELL ME WHY!!!*

I don't know if werewolves can understand each other's words; I never really tried speaking to any of the other freaks in the circus before, but right now I am shrieking at him all the questions I've had in my head for years. Hot tears stream all down my face as I rage at him. I just want him to tell me why...before I bloody murder him!

Funny how history tends to repeat, only this time he is the weakling, not me...I can't believe I used to be frightened by THIS pathetic excuse of a werewolf. When I was a child the villages of these lands were living in fear of 'The Beast of Dunninton', a werewolf that terrorised the moors and all around the moors. But if this is the Beast...then humans are more gutless than I thought. I am a younger female who is not even a pure blooded wolf, yet compared to me, my sire is an old mangy bag of bones with but only a few teeth, all of which are as blunt as butter-knives. I can understand why he'd appear scary to children; all animals bigger than children are scary to them. But I am not a child anymore...and I am almost ashamed that such a sham of a beast passed on his curse to me like a disease. The Dunninton Beast would prey on livestock and children (particularly young girls), and it's no wonder why; being this scrawny and cowardly, domestic animals and frail children were probably the only prey he could catch and overpower. Probably made him feel powerful and special. But the tables of karma have turned against him tonight.

This isn't even a fair fight; I'm twice his size and much stronger than him from all of the circus' dog-fights I survived. He is full of fear while I am now numb to fear due to my circus life. Thanks to my experience in killing my own kind, this weedy wolf never had a chance against his old chew-toy.

I don't bother using my claws or fangs because the mere force of my fists and kicks are enough to shatter the dog's bones, he is that weak and skinny. All the while I keep a tight hold of his tail...the same way he once kept hold of my hair while biting chunks out of my arms and shoulders. My whole hand wraps around his thin neck and squeezes as tight as it can go. His scraggly mane offers no protection whatsoever from my vice-like grip. He is struggling and choking, and I squeeze his neck tighter, but I squeeze much too tight and a sudden loud snap silences my sire forever.

His body goes limp and his now floppy head lolls unnaturally from my hand with his jaw sagging dumbly open. I've broken the bastard's neck. This has to be the easiest and quickest dog-fight I've ever won. Good riddance, the world is a much safer place without *you* in it anymore. I'm sure the spirits of all the other children whose innocence you also stole would agree with me as well. I am the new Beast of Dunninton now, and things are going to be a lot different around here from now on...but first there is one more thing I need to take care of. You see, it wasn't just you I remembered...I finally remember where my white cloak is, and I'm going to get it back, along with the rest of my life that was stolen from me.

I howl my anger and frustration to the moon. All that comes out of my maw is howling, but inside I am screaming out my rage as if I am trapped inside myself and crying out desperately for someone to hear me. For someone to save me from the beast that's swallowed me whole. The memories I've recovered bite my brain harder than any fangs of any wolf ever could...because nothing stings more than a broken heart. My heart was broken the night all of this horror started.

It was the end of spring. I was playing with my sister on these very moors; I remember it now, as if it were only yesterday. It makes sense now why I had my sister's cross, because we had swapped our trademark assets with one another as a prank. We spent all day pretending to be each other, fooling everyone into mistaking us for each other; we thought it was funny. Later we went to the moors to play in the flowerbeds...but we stayed out too late. We were having so much fun that we paid no attention to how dark the skies had gotten, so busy playing that we forgot what time of the month it was...and that was the biggest mistake of our lives. *He* found us. *He* hunted us. Being all alone so far away from our house; we were easy prey.

We ran but I fell behind, and when I fell he pounced on me. Pinned me down, grabbed my wrists and laid all of his weight on top of me to stop me squirming. It was the most frightening experience of my life, so frightening that I can't believe I forgot it. I had completely blocked it out of my mind...but perhaps the worst part of that moment was when I watched my sister run away without me. She didn't even look back. I cried out to her for help but she never came back for me. I felt so abandoned and confused, I swear I felt my heart tear in half beneath my breast, but fear overrode me as I felt his teeth and claws sink into me. I remember the pain so vividly; it was the first time I had ever felt such torturous agony, it hurt so much...I was screaming so loud that I'm surprised my lungs didn't burst. All I could think was *'I don't want to die'*.

I must've acted on instinct because I don't quite remember how I escaped him; all I remember is clutching my sister's crucifix and swinging it across his face, then hearing a surprised yowl. I honestly don't know how I found the strength and courage to get back up and flee, but I did. He never chased after me. I must've hurt his face really bad if he couldn't pursue me; that or he was such a coward that even a slap from a little girl would've sent him running away whimpering. But it did not mean I was safe. I was so scared and hurt that I had no idea where I'd run off to nor how far I had run. I ended up getting lost in a dense forest. I was afraid...no matter how loud I cried for my Mother and Father nobody came looking for me...nobody ever found me.

The rest is...a complete blur. I don't know how I survived for a full month all alone in a forest at such a young age with such horrible injuries. Maybe it was the curse passed on to me, keeping me alive. But I remember the heartache, the homesickness, the loneliness...and the hunger. The hunger was unbearable. I was so hungry...I ate whatever I could find or catch, from fruit and nuts to bugs and rotting animal carcasses. It was definitely the effect of the curse consuming me, making my hunger stronger and my tastes more...twisted. And then the big night came. My first full moon.

I was just a child so I had no clue about the curse...the pain of my first transformation was ten times worse than the attack a month ago. And a hundred times more terrifying. But once I had been fully engulfed by my new wolfish guise, all my reasoning and sanity was swallowed by my hunger. I was not me anymore. I had become a monster that just wore my skin. A monster that ate literally anything...and anyone. The moon changed me and I rampaged. On your first full moon you are out of control as your body tries to adjust to its new power and shape, but being alone and starved all month, I was driven mad. For three nights I ran amok in the forest, on the moors, and even around the farms and villages; butchering and devouring anything with a pulse. Many people died because of me...after I came back to my senses the morning after the third night of my first cycle, I had realised what I had done. My childhood was over, my life ruined, all because of our childish ignorance. Whoever came up with the old saying 'ignorance is bliss' really needs to try on my shoes, because it was 'bliss' that cost a lot of people's lives, including my own.

ACT VI

I waste no time in using the full moon's light to its full advantage as I take off at high speed with my new faster legs and larger lungs. What miles a human can run in a whole day, a wolf can run twice as many in just hours. My destination is a long one, so this month's full moon gives me the best opportunity to get there as quick as possible without detours or distractions. For the next two following nights I run along this one straight road, stopping only to drink when needed. I take a shortcut through a small wood I remember from my childhood to cut ahead of my journey. I'm going home.

It starts to rain tonight; softly at first but gradually it gets heavier and faster. My soaked fur is freezing the rest of me but I ignore the cold. It's not as if this is the first time the skies have pissed on me – at the circus I got rained on all the time whenever the keepers forgot to put a roof over my cage (which they forgot to do a LOT). The clowns would often piss on me through the bars after drinking too, but they stopped doing that after I sliced off one of their manhoods with my claws when the fool got too close. Rain didn't bother me back then and it won't bother me now.

It's now the last night of my cycle. I feel my body's strength waning a little but my blood boiling hotter; it's always like this on the last night...it's as if the wolf inside knows its time is coming to an end and it wants to make the most of it before the cycle finishes until next month. It's starving for more freedom and more hunting and just hates waiting every month. Just as well I reach my last stop and just in time too, just two hours before midnight. That's more than enough time to do what I plan to do.

I come to an abrupt halt in the shadows of the end of the woods facing my final destination. Before me stands the cottage from my memories...it's my family's house. It's still so hard for me to believe. I'm home, I'm really home. This isn't a wishful dream, I have really come back. The rain hides my tears very well but I feel their warmth on my hairy cheeks compared to the cold raindrops. This homely place is where I used to live with my Mother, Father, Grandfather...and twin sister.

I snarl at the thought of her now. This old cottage that once kept me safe and happy now torments me as it reminds me of all the years of love and happiness that could've, should've and would've been mine, if it was not for her. I shake my head clean of these thoughts and feelings. I mustn't let the wolf control me now; Mother and Father and Grandpa might be inside, and I cannot ever let them see me like this. If they find out what I am now...they'll send me back or even kill me. My Father's a forester so he has a gun; he'd shoot me dead...like he almost did before.

But still, the urge to get closer to take a peek at my home is far too tempting; I feel my big paws stalking towards the fence without me telling them to. I hide in the front garden's big flowerbed. Mother always let her phlox and veronica plants grow too tall; you could hide a treasure-chest in them, so I used to play hide and seek in them.

I look to the house's windows. All the lights are off bar two; one is in an upstairs room where my Grandpa used to sleep in and the other is shining through a downstairs' window where the living room is. My parents hated leaving the curtains open at night so, judging from the uncovered window, I'm guessing neither Mother nor Father is home. I creep up to the window and peer inside, and then I see *her*.

My sister, sat by the fire looking at a bunch of shopping catalogues and wearing my white cloak, the cloak my Grandpa bought for me. I growl and frown; how dare she keep wearing it all these years! It doesn't belong to her! And then I notice her looking excited at something in the pages. I watch her tear it out and I almost scream in outrage at what I spy her gleaming at. It's a ticket to go to a circus. MY circus.

This is the final straw; I've seen enough and so has the wolf. I don't give a damn about self-control anymore; the wolf can do what it wants right now, and in fact I encourage it to. After all, it is in my nature. So she wants to see a freakshow, does she? Well then, she doesn't need any ticket because the freakshow's star attraction has come to her.

I move to the front door and start pounding it with my fists angrily. I hear her short squeal of surprise from behind the wooden door then I hear her slowly approaching it. I can sense that she is hesitant to open the door to someone who's knocking so violently this late at night. She asks who's there before I hear her putting the door's chain up to keep the door secure in case of an attempted forced entry. It will take more than a lock and chain to keep the Big Bad Wolf out.

With a hideous snarl, I slam the door wide open with such brute force that I break both the lock and chain, and crack the wood. I tower over my trembling sister. I can barely squeeze through the small door, and my large frame blocks the whole entrance, thus preventing any attempts of passing me. The putrid smell of wet dog and vile animal-breath enters the room with me, and puddles of water gather around me on the carpet from my drenched fur as I barge my way into the house. I shake myself dry and water sprays all over the room, dousing the candles that kept the room alight. The only light now is that of the lit fireplace and the lightning outside.

Puffing out my muscular chest and standing as tall as I can to make myself look as huge as possible, I deliberately take my time stomping towards her – I want to savour the delectable fragrance of fear coming from her. My sister stumbles backwards, half paralysed with terror from the sight of a werewolf in her own home. You would think someone who's about to be killed would be staring at their killer's face or bloodied clothes, but no...The whole time her wide eyes are fixed on my neck.

I know what she's looking at: the crucifix on a chain around my mane, sparkling like a star each time it catches the light of the moon and lightning outside. She knows it's her crucifix, and I know she knows what that means; my snarl turns into a huge grin when she realises I know what she's thinking. She takes a shaky step back every time I take a step closer to her, until she is backed up into a corner. I have her trapped just where I want her: in a spot she cannot leave without getting caught by me. Since she can't get away from me, she now tries reaching behind her for anything she can use to defend herself with; a knife, a fire-poker, a broomstick, or even something to throw at me like a vase. But there is absolutely nothing within her reach to grab. She's both trapped and defenceless.

My sharp toothy grin stretches wider and then I slowly open my mouth, which by this point is overflowing with saliva in anticipation, teasing my prey wickedly. My cruel teasing proves to be very effective as I hear and smell urine soaking through her underwear and dripping onto the wooden floor. A rolling howl of triumph explodes out of my chest pass my yellow-white teeth and she cowers in response; I've heard that supposedly the last thing you do before you die is wet yourself and I just wanted to test that theory.

I have never managed to form even the simplest English words while being a wolf and I've tried countless times; even now I'm having trouble trying to make my beastly vocals sound the slightest bit human enough to be understandable...yet somehow my three words reach her and make her cry. *"Sister, I'm home."*

I lunge at her and she goes down under my weight, all but vanishing beneath me. I finally lose all control of myself and let instinct fully take over. With my ears deafened and my vision blurred with a mixture of instinctual savagery and boiling emotions, I tear, shred, crunch and crush whatever flesh my jaws can close around. Through it all she not once makes a single sound; she doesn't have the time or the energy to voice any fear, pain or protest. I suppose just witnessing my return alone is enough to destroy her before I could even touch her. Or maybe she has accepted her fate, as she knows that there is no one here to save her. But I don't want to kill her. I never did, I just want to be ME again...but I can't, because SHE is 'me'.

We are identical twins; nobody can tell us apart, not even our own parents. That is why Father didn't know who I was the first time I returned. I searched for the road home for three months after my first full moon. On my third full moon I finally found it and without thinking tried to follow it...but on my way I happened upon my sister. I was so happy to see her again, I ran to hug her but she screamed and ran from me.

At the time I was confused; yes I am a werewolf but surely as my sister she should recognise me and my clothes? I chased after her, begging her to stop and listen to me, but she kept running until somebody found us both. It was Father! I was even more overjoyed, especially when he called my name, but as I tried to approach he pointed his gun at me and yelled at me. I had never seen him so angry; was he mad because I hadn't come home? Did he hate me now that I was a wolf? *Dad I'm sorry...don't be scared, it's still me, I'm just a bit-* "STAY BACK, BEAST!" was the reply I got. I was scared now; I didn't know what to do. He didn't see me, he saw only the wolf. But he called my name...if he didn't know who I was, why did he call my name? But when he told me to get behind him...I realised what was going on when my sister ran to stand behind Father for protection. He was talking to her, not me.

My sister had stolen my name. She must've told our parents that it was her that the Dunninton Beast caught, and pretended to be me. Why, though? Why would my own sister do that to me? Was she scared she'd get into trouble for leaving me or something? I didn't understand. Father loaded fresh bullets into his shotgun and took aim. He was going to shoot me, and without my cloak he didn't know it was me. I cried. He then started to cry too. We were both crying, and then he snarled *"this is for taking my little girl away from me!"* He thought I was the Dunninton Beast. *No Daddy, please don't shoot me...she's not me! I'm me! It's me, I'm right here! So please Daddy, I'm not dead! Daddy NO!*

He fired at me. Shot me right in the neck, and then shot me again in the collarbone. I made no more noise; I fell to the ground painfully. I could feel the bullet stuck fast in my throat, choking me, but neither bullet was made of silver so they did not kill me. I passed out from both the lack of air and the pure agony. I didn't die but it felt like I had, because when I woke up I was in Hell. Four cage walls surrounding me on the back of a carriage transporting me to a new cruel life far, far away from home. Sold to the Circus like a tiger sold to a zoo. I still have one of the bullets lodged inside me you know; the one in my collarbone. I lost my memory of it at the circus but now it serves as a reminder of my sister's betrayal. The memories that the bullet holds are fresh in my mind again, but the one that drives me insane is the memory of my sister grinning and winking at me before I got shot.

A couple of hours pass before I eventually snap out of my fit of animalistic madness. My heart's still pounding like a drum and slowing my breathing does very little to help it relax. Coming out of a rage is almost therapeutic: you feel a sudden sense of calm and relief, and that's how I feel right now.

I rise up from my bloodied paws so that I am standing again. My sister is gone and I don't mean just dead, I mean completely gone. It's as though I have swallowed her whole all in one go (and while it might be only my imagination, I swear that I can feel wriggling and hear muffled groaning in my expanded belly as I speak). No body, no leftovers at all, just a big puddle of blood in the spot where she once stood, soaking into the wooden floorboards and my white cloak. A slightly amusing thought then flitters in my mind; now I can say my dearly departed sister will always be a part of me…and really mean it.

I don't know how in the world my cloak remained so intact after all that, with not so much as a rip in the cotton. How could my huge sharp claws swinging around so erratically possibly miss landing a single scratch on that thin fabric? And yet there it is, resting lifelessly on the floor, soaking up the red warm liquid; all that's left of the little deceiver who was wearing it only moments ago. It soaks up nearly all of the blood like a sponge, until there is just a large damp stain on the floor now. My cloak is no longer white either; now it is entirely red like a flattened rose but I don't mind. In fact I like this colour better than white anyway because white lies but blood is always true, and my cloak is now as red as blood.

I hear the clock chime twelve times. It is midnight; the power of the moon is starting to wane. When its grip on my soul loosens I can finally regain the capability to change back and forth at will. I close my eyes and force the wolf into submission, putting it away in its cage again until the next full moon, but this time the beast shows no resistance towards me. Its hunger for violence has been sated (for now). I open my eyes after my uncomfortable transformation; transforming back into a human is never a pleasant experience.

I unclasp the chain of my sister's crucifix necklace and remove it from my neck. I glare at it. I've worn it for years and I despise it now; spitefully I throw it out the open front door with such great force that it lands right into the garden's deep well, sinking in the deep dark water like a stone, never to be seen again. It's for the best. If anybody saw me wearing my dead sister's cross they'll wonder where I found it – it would raise suspicions.

After I shut the splintered door, I kneel down and pick up my cloak, then hang it up by the fire to dry it out; I rub my red hands together and hold them towards the fire. I sigh contentedly as the flames warm my flesh in a wonderful way. It's been years since I last sat beside a nice friendly fire; makes a delightful change from dirty thin blankets and damp mounds of mite-infested hay.

I look around my home. It's changed quite a bit; some furniture has been disposed of while some has been rearranged around the room, and there's new ornaments and decorations I've never seen before in here. Even the smell is different; I can't smell my Father's musky scent of cheap aftershave and whiskey anymore; instead I smell only my Mother's perfume and sister's expensive shampoo. Has Father died or divorced Mother or something?

But both my mind and body freeze when a voice calls my name from upstairs. My face lights up at the familiarity of the voice. It sounds like my Grandfather! I don my dry cloak to cover my naked breasts, and then ever so slowly and quietly I tip-toe up the stairs and turn left in the corridor where the door to my Grandfather's bedroom is. My heart is racing so fast and beating so hard with joy. I love my Grandfather very much. I have missed him terribly, and I cannot contain my excitement. Nevertheless, I resolve myself and carefully open the door and step inside...but my nose is instantly hit with a new smell that sadly I know all too well, and it kills my joy instantly. I see him, laying there in his bed with but only a single candle next to his bed to offer some means of light, breathing shallowly; his face is so pale. He is dying.

He struggles a little to open his eyes and turn his head in my direction. I start to wonder if he can see my sorry state; my cloak bleached crimson red, my trousers shredded and blood-stained, and my hair that was once a light chocolate colour now a long shaggy mess as black as the night sky itself. I hope not, I hope his poor eyesight and the shadows of the dimly lit room hide my current appearance. I don't want him to remember me this way...a killer and a cannibal. I want him to die remembering me as his granddaughter.

He brings out a trembling thin arm from underneath his thick duvet and his withering hand beckons me to come closer to him. I take a seat next to his bedside and hold his hand; it is so light in my palm but as warm as the fire downstairs, and I can feel it shaking with old age. I treasure its touch, the gentle hand of my beloved Grandfather. Tonight is surely the last time I'll ever hold it, so I want to hold onto it tightly for as long as possible.

He smiles at me weakly and I smile back, fighting the tears that threaten to leave my eyes. He asks what all that noise was downstairs and I am quick to make up a convincing lie; I tell him I was adding more logs of wood to the fire and accidentally dropped them when a stray dog howling outside startled me. He seems to believe it, but then he looks at my wrists when he feels the scars with his fingers and thumb. He asks with worry how I'd gotten such horrible scars but I don't answer him. I can't answer him, for there is no lie I can make that would be believable for the scars caused by tight iron cuffs and rusty chains.

He raises his gaze up to meet mine and asks me another question. "My dear, do you remember that song your Mama taught you?"

I nod my head. How could I ever forget it? I used to sing it all the time; it was my favourite lullaby. I used to even howl the tune of it at night, back at the circus.

"Please...won't you sing it for me? I've not heard you sing it for years."

Of course I've not sung it for so long, I have not been here to sing it and my sister was never a good singer; she would constantly forget the lyrics and get the tune wrong. I nod again and part my lips to let my song flow smoothly from deep inside me:

> *"Oh lonely moon, you look so cold;*
> *Yet why do you make me feel so warm?*
> *Oh lonely moon, how do you hold me;*
> *When you have no open arms?*
> *Oh lonely moon, you are my only light;*
> *And how I wish I could be yours.*

Oh lonely moon, you're so beautiful;
It's your radiant glow my heart most adores.
Oh lonely moon, you are so silent;
So I shall sing for you.
Oh lonely moon, won't you sing too?
Sing, sing with me oh bright moon;
I raise my head up high to you.
I sing for you tonight, as I do every night;
Crescent or full, over you I still will swoon;
For I love you, my oh so lonely moon."

When I finish my song the rain outside dies down and the thunder ceases. I see him start to cry then I also begin to cry with him. His smile widens and before I can say anything he says only one last sentence. "I have missed you so much." And then...his hand becomes limp in mine, and his head sinks back into his pillow with one last breath as his eyes close forever, never to open again. He is gone.

I am speechless. He missed me? Does that mean...he's known all this time? *Oh Grandpa, I've missed you too...I love you Grandpa, rest in peace and I pray that you'll forgive me for all the evil I have done.*

I fall forward onto his blanketed corpse and cry into his still chest with all my heart. I made it. Thank god I made it home; I made it just in time to say a final goodbye. It has been so long since I saw his kind smile that I forgot who I was and where I came from. But I never forgot our lullaby, the lullaby he sang for his daughter who in turn sung it to her daughters; the same lullaby I just sang now to lull him into an everlasting peaceful sleep.

I quake with each sob. I feel so lost now, even more lost than on the first night of my curse. I am alive and free, but what now? Where do I go from here? Then without thinking I howl softly to the setting moon outside the window; a long mournful howl that lasts until the first ray of dawn to bring forth the morning of a fresh new start and the end of my nightmare.

FINALE

It is so strange, my life to me now. I feel so hollow inside, as if a part of me left this world with my sister and Grandfather. Even after returning home and reuniting with what is left of my family, I am still haunted by vivid nightmares. So many years of nothing but darkness; so much fear and sadness all that time. I'm trying to move on but I just can't seem to let go of the memories; then again, I can't imagine anybody being able to.

Circus Grimm is gone for good, but a piece of me refuses to accept that. Deep down I still feel like it's too good to be true, even though it is true. It's impossible for me to ever be whole again after so much loss; I have lost my grace and innocence. Oh how I wish I could just turn back the pages of time and relive the happier days of my past, to have another chance to live the life that was stolen from me, but alas I am a werewolf, not a genie. I'll forever wonder what I did so wrong that I deserved all that's happened to me, but I know I'll never get an answer. I have learnt the very hard way that sometimes bad things just happen for no reason, no matter whether you're good or bad, an animal or a man, woman, elder or child…and when they do happen, they change you, for better or for worse.

It wasn't too difficult resettling back into my true identity like I originally expected though. Because we looked and sounded alike as twins, nobody really noticed any changes from neither my return nor my sister's disappearance, especially since neither of us had many friends with us living deep in the woods, so far away from the village that Mother and Father ran a market-stall in. Of course, I still had to be careful when I was learning what my sister had been up to during my absence; people would find it very strange if someone they knew suddenly had an inexplicable loss of memory.

I learned that my sister had taken over the stall for Mother so now I had a new job when I came home, but I'm not complaining – it's easy work and takes my mind off my past. And quite frankly I'll pick getting paid to work in a busy market over getting forced to work in a circus any day. I'm glad to say that I will never miss being a 'star', not ever. It's actually a little ironic because I remember that I always wanted to be a famous actress when I was a child…my wish partially came true in a dark twisted way, but there was no greener grass on the other side, no grass at all in fact, just mud and gravel. I was famous but I wasn't an actress. I was on show but in a cage, not on a stage. I literally made a living by killing; people knew only my title, not my name. I was basically a show-dog…Far cry from actress. I never wanted any of that. I never wanted to be a werewolf and I still don't, but what we want to be and what we become are as different as sand and ash.

The world is full of 'Ringmasters' and 'Dunninton Beasts' skulking in the dark crevices of society, who live only to cause the suffering and misery of others. Hateful people like them prey on the innocent for their own selfish gain, with little to no regard for the damage they cause. And their selfishness and malevolence are contagious; they infect your spirit like an incurable disease. They fill you with a darkening hate that slowly becomes a part of you, and pain and hatred make you do things you never thought you could ever do; sometimes very terrible things. There is an inner beast in all of us; that nagging in your head when there's something you want, that tingling in your gut when you sense something's wrong, that urge to just run away or lash out when stressed – it is the animal inside us crying to be let out…and feeding it with hatred is NOT advisable. That's what happened to me and look what it brought me. So you need to be careful what future you wish for, because in life you rarely get what you want.

I never did find out what happened to my Father. Mother doesn't talk about him at all and when I tried asking why she just cried, so I probed no further for answers after that…I had to accept that I will most likely never see him again. I continued living in that cottage with my Mother for a while, but I might as well have been living with a zombie...my 'death' (or rather my sister's) years ago had destroyed her spirit; she never spoke a word of her ever again it seemed. She had tried to pretend she only had one daughter in an effort to heal her broken heart. It's hard to believe that all this grief and horror was caused by that one miserable excuse of an animal called the Dunninton Beast. One bite was all it took to ruin so many lives. I wanted to tell her so many times that the bastard is dead, that I avenged us all by killing him. Keeping such a triumph hidden away ripped at my sides...but it is a secret I must take to my grave. Mother has suffered enough; it would kill her if she ever found out what truly happened to her daughters.

A few days ago I noticed an article in the village's newspapers when I was shopping for Mother. It was about Circus Grimm; in fine detail it told how the ruins of the burnt circus were discovered by corn harvesters just weeks after the fire. There had been no survivors (or so they believed). The Landlord was arrested shortly after the *grim* discovery; he was trialled and hanged for arson and murder. There was very little mention of my victims though; apparently the fire had erased most of the evidence of my play in the mutinous plot, but the article made the public aware that some of the circus' animals and freaks might've escaped. If the shopkeeper wasn't watching me reading the article I would smirk and maybe chuckle. This means I'm as good as dead to the authorities; thanks to the fire, the main star of the Freak Show had vanished without a trace. This means nobody will be looking for me and for once I don't want anyone to find me. I really am free now; free from the suffering of my hellish home in Circus Grimm, and free from the real truth about circus life for animals and freaks that nobody will ever know…

As time passed I noticed the gradual decrease in number of circuses and other traveling performing troupes around these lands. It's as if they have become cursed grounds for them now; they have become too fearful of whatever ghosts could be haunting the burned down circus' resting place, or what surviving monsters could be lurking in the maze of cornfields that have been left unharvested ever since the finding of Circus Grimm's scorched remains. New laws on circuses started mysteriously coming into action too; the usage of animals of any kind in circuses was abolished and 'freaks' were no longer allowed. They say it's because people thought it was barbaric and inhumane, but I'm no fool...I know the truth. They are scared of me. The Circus Wolfman that escaped. They don't want history to repeat – that's the real reason for these new laws, but as if they'll ever admit that.

Many moons have risen and fallen since then. I am a traveller myself now, never staying in the same place for too long and I hardly ever visit my family's old cottage these days. I've long since lost track of my age; it's been years or perhaps centuries and I still don't look much older than what I did the night I returned home. I'm not quite sure how long a werewolf is meant to live for. Hundreds of years? Thousands of years? Maybe forever. I don't know. There's not exactly an encyclopaedia for lycanthropy to study with.

I like to believe that one day I will finally be granted my eternal rest; everything that has a beginning must also have an ending, mustn't it? There is no author who writes endlessly, no monarch who rules eternally…and no show that performs forever. Have I continued being a killer though, I hear you ask? Unfortunately so…but it's not as if I don't try to avoid doing it. I always stay deep in the woods or lock myself up when the full moon comes. I never deliberately hunt humans and always roar at them to scare them away from me if I do see any, but when humans hunt you or get in the way of your prey…well, sadly accidents happen; it cannot be helped. And I always pray for the humans I do end up slaying. I do feel guilt and sorrow for them; after all, I used to be human once…I am an animal now but not a monster. Not anymore.

I no longer try to defy the full moon. I am what I am and must live with that. When I gaze at the night sky now and watch the moon fatten then wane then fatten again, I don't try to hide from it behind curtains like I used to. I'm not scared of what the moon does to me anymore. However, I am unlike any other wolf now. My past has made it impossible for me to join any packs or find a mate, and I am far too used to fighting and killing my own species to make any means of peaceful interactions with any other wolves. My hate for the Beast of Dunninton has also twisted my perception of my brethren; if I stumble upon the territory of another werewolf who is anything like him, I tear that wolf limb from limb. I do the exact same to any circuses I come across; I either snap and obliterate the whole place, or I break open the cages of any animals and/or freaks I see. I guess it is not just my body that is scarred but also my mind. I make a reputation for myself in every land I journey to; other werewolves will either abandon their turfs or try to drive me out, and humans put a bounty on my head like they would for a famous wanted criminal.

They remember what I did to my circus, but over the years the story has changed so much. Facts have been lost and invented over time. Some versions of my tale you may remember from your childhood. I have become what you would call an urban legend of sorts. People give me so many different names: the Dunninton Beast, the Reaper's Pet, the Beast on the Moors, the King of Wolves, Prince of the Night, The Wolf in Red Clothing, The Big Bad Wolf (admittedly my personal favourite), and much more. But no matter what name they give me or what version of my story they tell, they all describe the same entity; a giant ghostly wolf as black as the darkest night with fearless eyes, scarred wrists and a howl that sounds eerily like a haunting song, and around its mane a small tattered cloak as red as blood.

So if you hear my howl, run all the way home. If you see a wolf in a red cloak, please leave it be. I will not bite so long as you don't pick a fight. The next time you visit a circus please remember my tale, and never go to a circus on a full moon. And this final warning is most important for all troupes out there who do not want to end up just like Circus Grimm: treat all your all performers fairly and be sure to keep no animals, not even horses...*or the Circus Wolfman might just pay your troupe a little visit!*

THE END

AFTERWORD

Thank you for reading my story 'The Circus Wolfman' and I hope you enjoyed it. I am Francine Woodward, a horror/fantasy artist in England who specialises in illustrating, animation and costuming. This is my first ever novella, and it was actually a job I was wearing my icon costume 'The Werewolf of West Yorkshire' for that sparked the idea for this story; I was doing a scare-acting job for Hallowscream at York Maze which has a circus freakshow theme for part of the attraction. During my lunch break I would doodle on some scrap paper to pass time; the drawings came out pretty well and it was pretty fun to do so I kept at it, and I even drew at my full time job whenever I got bored (and when my employer wasn't looking). I started uploading the drawings onto my websites regularly and was surprised by how many people liked them and their theme. They asked for more and before I knew it a story was born. My story was supposed to have a hidden message about animal-abuse in old circuses and contain a teeny tiny reference to the Little Red Riding Hood tale, but without me realising it the story soon started also symbolising slavery, discrimination, dog-fighting, and severe psychological damage caused by traumatic experiences (particularly murder, bullying and sexual assault)…and then ultimately breaking free from it all and slowly recovering, albeit with great difficulty and not without leaving scars. I honestly did not even notice my story was representing all these 'grim' topics until several of my supporters who first saw and read quotes from the story pointed it out to me, but I suppose that's the beauty of werewolves and one of the reasons why I love them; they are one of fiction's greatest enigmas and the best metaphor for the destructive side of human nature.

Printed in Great Britain
by Amazon